POCKET
GOOD
GUIDES

BEST
HOTELS FOR
BUDGET
FLYERS

GOOD GUIDES

POCKET GOOD GUIDES

BEST HOTELS FOR BUDGET FLYERS

EDITED BY DESMOND BALMER

EBURY PRESS

First published in Great Britain in 2004
Ebury Press
Random House
20 Vauxhall Bridge Road
London SW1 2SA

10 9 8 7 6 5 4 3 2 1

Random House Australia (Pty) Limited
20 Alfred Street, Milsons Point
Sydney
New South Wales 2061, Australia

Random House New Zealand Limited
18 Poland Road, Glenfield, Auckland 10
New Zealand

Random House South Africa (Pty) Limited
Endulini, 5A Jubilee Road
Parktown 2193
South Africa

Random House UK Limited Reg. No. 954009

www.randomhouse.co.uk

A CIP catalogue record for this book is available from the British Library

ISBN 0 09 189 6681

Papers used by Ebury Press are natural, recyclable products made from wood
grown in sustainable forests

Typeset by Textype, Cambridge
Cover design by Lim at Nim Design
Printed and bound in Denmark by Nørhaven Paperback, Viborg

Introduction

It may be easy to find a cheap flight on the Internet. It is altogether harder to find the right place to stay. You can never be certain of the quality of the hotels listed on budget airline websites, which are commercial selections by outside agencies. This pocket guide provides an independent view, with a selection of more than 200 tried-and-tested hotels from the authoritative database of the *Good Hotel Guide*.

We have selected hotels for all the main European destinations served by the low-cost airlines. They come in all shapes and sizes, including simple B&Bs, country inns at budget prices, and hip designer hotels. The selection includes city hotels, which can be reached by public transport, and some wonderful rural places within reasonable driving distance, if you choose to hire a car. What they have in common is that they have all been recommended and checked out by *Good Hotel Guide* inspectors or readers. Unlike some rival guides, the hotels do not pay to be included and the editors and staff do not accept hospitality.

The *Good Hotel Guide* is often described as word-of-mouth in print; the entries, enlivened by quotations from our correspondents, will give you an insight into what it is like to stay in these hotels. We believe this pocket guide will help you find a hotel that fulfils your requirements. Happy travelling.

Desmond Balmer

How to read the entries

These entries are shortened versions of the listings provided in the 2004 editions of the *Good Hotel Guide*. We have concentrated on the information that best communicates the flavour of each hotel. The quotations come from the reports of inspectors and readers of the Continental and GB & Ireland editions of the *Guide*.

We have focussed on the facilities that will be of particular interest to the short-break traveller. The directions for city hotels are given in relation to the city centre. We try to be accurate with the directions for those hotels in rural locations where car hire will be necessary; we suggest that you will still need a good road map for some of the out-of-the-way hotels.

Most of the hotels in this Guide are within the Euro-zone and the prices are quoted in Euros. Some hotels outside the Euro-zone also quote their prices in Euros; where they don't, we quote the prices in local currency. The exchange rates are subject to fluctuation; it is best to check the exact rates at the time of booking.

Hotel tariffs are complicated. The figures given without mention of a single or double room are per person for bed and breakfast (B&B) or dinner, bed and breakfast (D,B&B); otherwise we quote a room rate. We give the D,B&B rate where possible; otherwise we quote the price of set meals. We cannot guarantee the tariffs given here. They were the prices quoted for at least part of 2004 at the time of going to press. Always check with the hotel at the time of booking.

Contents

The airlines

These are the low-cost airlines whose routes are featured in this guide.

Air Berlin
www.airberlin.com, 0870 738 88 80.

bmibaby
www.bmibaby.com, 0870 264 2229.

easyJet
www.easyjet.com, 0871 7 500 100.

FlyBE
www.flybe.com, 0871 700 0535.

German Wings
www.germanwings.com, 01805 955 855.

Jet2
www.jet2.com, 0870 737 8282.

MyTravelLite
www.mytravellite.com, 08701 564 564.

Ryanair
www.ryanair.com, 0871 246 0000.

Thomsonfly
www.thomsonfly.com, 0870 1900 737.

Sky Europe
www.skyeurope.com, 020 7365 0365.

Volareweb
www.volareweb.com, 0800 032 0992.

From an airport near you

The low-cost revolution is not confined to Stansted and Luton. There are a growing number of cheap flights to European destinations from regional airports across the UK. Listed here, by airport and airline, are the main direct low-cost routes. Low-cost airlines are notoriously fickle and can axe destinations at short notice. You can check the latest route information on airline and airport websites.

Aberdeen (www.baa.com)
FlyBE to Paris.
Ryanair to Dublin.

Belfast City Airport (www.belfastcityairport.com)
FlyBE toToulouse.

Belfast International Airport (www.belfastairport.com)
easyJet to Amsterdam.
Jet2 to Prague.

Birmingham (www.bhx.co.uk)
FlyBE to Cork, Graz, Perpignan, Salzburg, Shannon, Toulouse.
MyTravelLite to Alicante, Almería, Barcelona, Dublin, Faro, Knock, Málaga, Palma, Tenerife.
Ryanair to Dublin, Girona.

Blackpool (www.blackpoolairport.com)
Ryanair to Dublin.

Bournemouth (www.flybournemouth.com)
Ryanair to Dublin, Girona.

Bristol (www.bristolairport.co.uk)
easyJet to Alicante, Amsterdam, Barcelona, Berlin, Bilbao, Copenhagen, Faro, Málaga, Nice, Palma, Prague, Venice.
FlyBE to Bergerac, Bordeaux, Paris, Toulouse.
Ryanair to Dublin.

Cardiff (www.cardiffairportonline.com)
bmibaby to Alicante, Cork, Geneva, Málaga, Milan, Palma, Paris, Prague, Toulouse.
Ryanair to Dublin.

Coventry (www.coventry-airport.co.uk)
Thomsonfly to Málaga, Marseille, Naples, Nice, Palma, Pisa, Rome, Venice.

Edinburgh (www.baa.com)
easyJet to Amsterdam.
FlyBE to Cork, Paris, Shannon, Toulouse.
German Wings to Cologne.
Ryanair to Dublin.

Exeter (www.exeter-airport.co.uk)
FlyBE to Alicante, Dublin, Faro, Málaga.

Gatwick (www.baa.com)
easyJet to Alicante, Amsterdam, Barcelona, Bilbao, Faro, Geneva, Málaga, Marseille, Milan, Naples, Nice, Palma, Prague, Toulouse.
FlyBE to Bordeaux, Nantes, Strasbourg.
Ryanair to Dublin.

Glasgow International (www.baa.com)
easyJet to Amsterdam.
FlyBE to Cork, Shannon, Toulouse.

Glasgow Prestwick (www.glasgow.pwk.com)
Ryanair to Brussels, Dublin, Frankfurt/Hahn, Girona, Gothenburg, Milan, Oslo, Paris, Shannon, Stockholm.

Leeds Bradford (lbia.co.uk)
Jet2 to Alicante, Amsterdam, Barcelona, Faro, Geneva, Málaga, Nice, Palma, Prague, Venice.
Ryanair to Dublin.

Liverpool (www.liverpooljohnlennonairport.com)
easyJet to Alicante, Amsterdam, Barcelona, Berlin, Geneva, Málaga, Nice, Palma, Paris.
Ryanair to Dublin, Girona.

Luton (www.london-luton.co.uk)
easyJet to Alicante, Amsterdam, Barcelona, Berlin, Budapest, Faro, Geneva, Málaga, Nice, Palma, Paris, Zürich.
Ryanair to Dublin, Milan.
Volareweb to Cagliari, Venice.

Manchester (www.manchesterairport.com)
Bmibaby to Alicante, Barcelona, Bordeaux, Cork, Geneva, Knock, Málaga, Palma, Paris, Prague.
FlyBE to Paris.
MyTravelLite to Tenerife.

Newcastle (www.newcastleairport.com)
easyJet to Alicante, Barcelona, Berlin, Copenhagen, Málaga, Nice, Palma, Paris, Prague.
Ryanair to Dublin.

Nottingham East Midlands (www.eastmidlandsairport.com)
bmibaby to Alicante, Amsterdam, Barcelona, Bordeaux, Cork, Dublin, Faro, Geneva, Málaga, Milan, Nice, Palma, Paris, Prague, Toulouse.
easyJet to Alicante, Barcelona, Faro, Geneva, Málaga, Prague, Venice.

Southampton (www.baa.com)
FlyBE to Alicante, Bergerac, Chambéry, Dublin, Geneva, Limoges, Málaga, Paris, Perpignan, Prague, La Rochelle, Salzburg, Toulouse.

Stansted (www.baa.com)
Air Berlin to Berlin, Düsseldorf, Palma.
easyJet to Alicante, Amsterdam, Barcelona, Bilbao, Bologna, Copenhagen, Faro, Lyon, Málaga, Milan, Munich, Naples, Nice, Palma, Prague, Rome, Venice.
German Wings to Cologne.
Ryanair to Aarhus, Alghero, Altenburg, Ancona, Bari, Bergerac, Berlin, Biarritz, Bologna, Brest, Brussels, Carcassonne, Cork, Dinard, Dublin, Düsseldorf, Eindhoven, Esbjerg, Frankfurt/Hahn, Friedrichshafen, Genoa, Girona, Gothenburg, Graz, Groningen, Hamburg/Lübeck, Jerez, Karlsruhe/Baden, Kerry, Klagenfurt, Knock, Limoges, Milan, Montpellier, Nîmes, Oslo, Palermo, Pau, Perpignan, Pisa, Poitiers, Reus, La Rochelle, Rodez, Rome, Salzburg, Shannon, St-Étienne, Stockholm, Tours, Treviso, Trieste, Valladolid, Verona Brescia.
Sky Europe to Budapest.

Teesside (www.teessideairport.com)
bmibaby to Alicante, Geneva, Málaga, Nice, Palma, Prague.

AUSTRIA

GRAZ
(FlyBE, Ryanair)

The airport is 5 km south of the city.

SCHLOSSBERG HOTEL   stylish

Kaiser-Franz-Josef-Kai 30
Graz
8010 Steiermark

Tel 00 43 316 80700
Fax 00 43 316 807070
Email office@schlossberg-hotel.at
Website www.schlossberg-hotel.at

Painted blue, this old building, in the centre of Graz, has been turned by its architect owner, Dr Helmut Marko, into a stylish B&B hotel. 'Beautifully renovated and furnished', it has beamed and vaulted ceilings, rambling corridors, country-style antiques and traditional fabrics, modern and old paintings, inner courtyards and terraced gardens. A visitor reports: 'Our small bedroom, with lovely pine wardrobe and good marbled bathroom, was like a small suite.' Breakfast can be served in the 'lovely' winter garden. There is a rooftop terrace with a small swimming pool and city views. Many restaurants nearby.

Open All year, except Christmas/New Year. **Rooms** 4 suites, 50 double. **Facilities** Lift. Reception/lounge, clubroom, bar, breakfast room/conservatory; wellness room, solarium. **Location** 5 mins' walk from centre. **Credit cards** All major cards accepted. **Terms** B&B: single €102–€305, double €146–€375.

HOTEL BURG BERNSTEIN   historic

Schlossweg 1   *Tel* 00 43 3354 6382
Bernstein   *Fax* 00 43 3354 6520
7434 Burgenland   *Email* burgbernstein@netway.at
                                      Website www.burgbernstein.at

Drive out into the rolling wooded hills in Bergenland, near the Hungarian border, to experience a traditional Austrian welcome from the family of Count Lázlo Almásy, of *The English Patient* fame. The family home is an imposing fortress whose history spans 800 years, though the current building dates almost entirely from the 17th century. Despite stuccoed ceilings, flagstone floors, huge fireplaces and stone staircase, paintings and antiques, it is not grand. Alexander and Andrea Berger-Almásy say that guests are received 'as members of the family', and 'should not expect the standard of a four- or five-star hotel'. He welcomes visitors, carries cases, serves at table; she produces a simple no-choice dinner, in a 'splendid banqueting hall', lit only by candles, and with Renaissance hunting friezes. The large bedrooms have no telephone, TV, minibar or door key; heating is mostly by antique wood-burning stoves. Best visited in summer; in winter, the castle operates as a B&B only.

Open All year. Dining room closed Oct–May, and midday. **Rooms** 6 suites, 4 double. **Facilities** Ramps. Salon, lounge, bar, dining room; chapel; sauna. 16-hectare park: garden, unheated swimming pool. **Location** Take the A2 from Graz towards Vienna. Exit at junction 111 to Oberwart; B57 to Bernstein. The castle is 300 m above village. **Credit cards** All major cards accepted. **Terms** B&B double €160–€262. Set dinner €33.

KLAGENFURT
(Ryanair)

The airport, close to the town,
is the gateway to Carinthia.

HOTEL DIE FORELLE   lakeside

Fischergasse 65   *Tel* 00 43 477 6620500
Millstatt am See   *Fax* 00 43 477 205011
9872 Kärnten   *Email* office@hotel-forelle.at
                         Website www.hotel-forelle.at

Mathias and Christa Aniwanter's long-established family hotel has a delightful position, on a promontory on the lake, in this quiet and friendly resort some 70 km from Klagenfurt. They keep a 'watchful eye on proceedings'. An enthusiastic visitor reports: 'It is one of my favourites in all Europe. There is a splendid dining terrace, a small outdoor pool, a sun terrace, a delightful bar, and an excellent restaurant: don't miss the fillet of rabbit. The service is first rate.' Bedrooms are spacious, and most have a 'wonderful' balcony looking over the lake. Upper Millstatt, five minutes' drive away, has spectacular views.

Open May–Oct. **Rooms** 60. **Facilities** Lounges, bar, restaurant; dining terrace; beauty treatments. Garden: sun terrace, swimming pool, beach. **Location** On lake. NW of Klagenfurt, 4 km E of Seeboden. **Credit cards** MasterCard, Visa. **Terms** D,B&B €67–€132.50. No single surcharge in low season.

SCHLOSS LEONSTAIN   gourmet

Hauptstrasse 228   *Tel* 00 43 4272 28160
Pörtschach am Wörthersee   *Fax* 00 43 4272 2823
9210 Kärnten   *Email* info@leonstain.at
                                   Website www.leonstain.at

Christoph Neuscheller has converted this white former monastery into a sophisticated hotel/restaurant. It stands on the main street of a fashionable Wörthersee resort west of Klagenfurt, and has lawns at the side and rear. 'Truly charming; delightful staff,' was one comment. There are wooden beams and white walls, pictures and antiques. Bedrooms are stylish: 'Ours, quirkily shaped, had an alcove, an antique chest, yellow fabrics, a balcony with chairs and tables, a good bathroom with under-floor heating.' From some rooms you can hear the railway at the back. The modern cuisine in the formal restaurant, with its minimalist decor, is thought 'excellent'. Breakfast is mainly DIY. In summer, meals are served by a fountain, under vine-covered trellises, in the arcaded courtyard graced by a bust of Brahms, who once stayed when it was a monastery. On the other side of the road is a private grassy beach, with sailing boats, parasols, bathing in the lake's cool, clear water, and views of snow-capped mountains.

Open May–Oct. **Rooms** 5 suites, 25 double, 2 single. **Facilities** Bar, restaurant; games room; sauna, solarium, cure centre. Courtyard, garden; private beach across road (summer restaurant). Golf nearby. **Location** Main street of resort. 20 km W of Klagenfurt. Parking. **Credit cards** Diners, MasterCard, Visa. **Terms** B&B €69–€139; D,B&B €19–€25 added per person.

SALZBURG
(FlyBE, Ryanair)

The airport is 4 km south of the city.

ALTSTADTHOTEL WEISSE TAUBE   value

Kaigasse 9
5020 Salzburg

Tel 00 43 662 842404
Fax 00 43 662 841783
Email hotel@weissetaube.at
Website www.weissetaube.at

A 14th-century *Burgerhaus* in an 'outstanding' location, near the Mozartplatz. It was converted into a *Gasthaus* in 1809 and has been in the hands of the same family since 1904. Doris and Helmut Wollner, the fourth-generation owners, are 'friendly', staff are efficient. 'Bedrooms are simple but pleasant,' say visitors. 'Highly recommended. Good breakfast (not a buffet): extras at reasonable cost.'

Open All year. **Rooms** 25 double, 6 single. **Facilities** Lift. Breakfast room. **Location** Central, near Mozartplatz. Street parking nearby. **Credit cards** All major cards accepted. **Terms** B&B: single €61–€82, double €95–€165.

GASTHOF-HOTEL DOKTORWIRT   old inn

Glaser Strasse 9
5026 Salzburg-Aigen

Tel 00 43 662 6229730
Fax 00 43 662 62171725
Email schnoell@doktorwirt.co.at
Website www.doktorwirt.co.at

'Very comfortable, with excellent service, splendid food with plenty of choice.' This old inn is in a residential suburb, ten minutes by bus from the centre. With much panelling, beamed ceilings and carved wooden furniture, it dates back to the 12th century. It is run by the 'extremely helpful' Karl and Anneliese Schnöll (his family have owned it for over a century). Their identical twin daughters and younger son help their parents, 'working indefatigably', says a visitor. 'You can combine visits to the city with a relaxing setting against wooded hills.' In summer, the swimming pool in the garden provides relief from the heat of the city. Some bedrooms have a balcony. Also liked are the 'delightful dogs'. Breakfast is in a conservatory; a three-course set lunch and a simple dinner menu are offered. The Von Trapp family home is nearby.

Open All year, except 2nd/3rd week Feb, mid-Oct–end Nov. Restaurant closed Mon, and Sun low season. **Rooms** 4 junior suites, 29 double, 6 single. **Facilities** Bar, 3 *Stüberl* (1 no-smoking), restaurant, conservatory. Garden: terrace. **Location** 4 km S of centre (10 mins by bus). **Credit cards** All major cards accepted. **Terms** B&B: single €65–€85, double €105–€160; D,B&B €15 added per person; full board €30 added per person.

BELGIUM

BRUSSELS
(Ryanair)

Ryanair flies to Charleroi, which is 60 km south.

STANHOPE HOTEL   **luxury**

Rue du Commerce 9   *Tel* 00 32 2 506 91 11
1000 Brussels   *Fax* 00 32 2 512 17 08
Email summithotels@stanhope.be
Website www.stanhope.be

A turn-of-the-century town residence, once a small town house hotel, given a make-over as a luxury hotel. 'A lovely place; old-fashioned quality and service, with all mod cons underneath,' says a visitor. 'My sensibly sized room had a blissfully comfortable bed, good lighting, and a great bathroom, with stylish mirrors and a decent shower. Nice touches like free shoe-cleaning. Not cheap, but quiet and recommended.'

Open All year. **Rooms** 43 suites, 43 double, 9 single. **Facilities** 2 lounges, bar, restaurant. Garden. **Location** Central, near Royal Palace. **Credit cards** All major cards accepted. **Terms** B&B: single from €140, double from €150, suite from €255. Set meals from €37; full alc €50.

HOTEL REMBRANDT   budget

42 rue de la Concorde   *Tel* 00 32 2 512 71 39
1050 Brussels   *Fax* 00 32 2 511 71 36
                                         Email rembrandt@brutele.be

'I never cease to be amazed at the value,' says a regular visitor to the Grasset-Gallais family's modest but 'professionally run' B&B, 'superbly located' just off the Avenue Louise. 'Every room is spotless; those with shower and loo are spacious; a marvellous collection of old photographs and/or jigsaws of Old Masters adorns the walls.' Jacqueline Grasset, 'formal and polite', is the manager: 'She is anxious to know when you will check in; if warned, she is prepared to emerge in her dressing gown to let you in as midnight approaches.' A large dresser separates the sitting room/reception from the breakfast area: 'Breakfast may be fairly basic, but the bread is always fresh, and the service punctilious.' The street is quiet at night; on weekdays there can be traffic noise quite early.

Open 5 Jan–5 Aug, 25 Aug–20 Dec. **Rooms** 12 double, 1 single. **Facilities** Small lift. Sitting room, breakfast room (no-smoking). **Location** Off Ave Louise, near Pl Stéphanie. (Metro: Place Louise, Porte de Namur) **Credit cards** All major cards accepted. **Terms** B&B: single €39–€65, double €65–€90.

LE DIXSEPTIÈME   historic

Rue de la Madeleine 25   *Tel* 00 32 2 502 57 44
1000 Brussels   *Fax* 00 32 2 502 64 24
                                 Email info@ledixseptieme.be
                                 Website www.ledixseptieme.be

Once the home of the Spanish ambassador, this B&B has a 'wonderful' location, opposite a church in a side street between the Grand'Place and the central station. Two readers hold contrasting views. 'The only place to stay in Brussels,' said a returning visitor. 'Wonderful suite the size of a London flat; accommodating service, exquisite breakfasts.' Most guests find the place 'glamorous' and 'stylish', but a dissenter was disappointed: 'Our junior suite (the second-cheapest) had a large but gloomy sitting room, comfortable, not elegant, a tiny bedroom with bare boards and fitted wardrobes, no furniture apart from the bed, a good bathroom.' The bedrooms are all different, some period (one has a *trompe l'œil* mural), some modern. Earlier visitors liked the 'old-world' feel, the free Internet access, the 'beautiful parlour where I had tea, pretty carved wooden staircase, lovely breakfast room' (where a 'good hot and cold buffet' is served). Front rooms get street noise.

Open All year. **Rooms** 12 suites, 12 double. **Facilities** Lift. Lobby, bar, breakfast room; conference room. Courtyard. **Location** Central, near Grand'Place. Public car park nearby. **Restrictions** No smoking: restaurant, bedrooms. **Credit cards** All major cards accepted. **Terms** B&B: single €180–€410, double €200–€430.

CZECH REPUBLIC

PRAGUE

(bmibaby, easyJet, FlyBE, Jet2)

The airport is 16 km north-west of the city.

HOTEL 16   value

Katerinská 16   *Tel* 00 420 2 24 92 06 36
128 00 Prague 2   *Fax* 00 420 2 24 92 06 26
                                 Email hotel16@hotel16.cz
                                 Website www.hotel16.cz

A small B&B hotel near the botanical gardens – 'so welcoming you wouldn't want to stay anywhere else'. It has a skylit atrium and a pleasant, terraced rear garden: bedrooms looking over this are 'absolutely quiet'. Other comments: 'The multilingual staff were our source for all kinds of information, and they completely won us over when they offered our children refreshments while they waited for us to return with our car after checking out). 'Good buffet breakfast.' Wenceslas Square and the 'wonderful' *Café Slavia* on the riverbank are about ten minutes' walk away. 'Reasonably priced.'

Open All year. **Rooms** 14. **Facilities** Breakfast room. Garden. Antique shop. **Location** 1 km SW of Wenceslas Square. Parking. Airport transfer (book in advance). **Credit cards** MasterCard, Visa. **Terms** B&B: single 2,500 Kč, double 2,700–3,400 Kč, junior suite 3,200–4,600 Kč.

HOTEL HOFFMEISTER   luxury

Pod Bruskou 7
118 00 Prague 1

Tel 00 420 2 51 01 71 11
Fax 00 420 2 51 01 71 20
Email hotel@hoffmeister.cz
Website www.hoffmeister.cz

This stylish white-fronted hotel (Relais & Châteaux) is near the left bank of the river Vltava, on a busy boulevard below the castle, in the Malá Strana district of offices, embassies and smart restaurants. Street-facing rooms have double glazing; there is a flowery inner courtyard where meals can be served, and in summer, the *Café Ria* (offering light meals) opens on to a terrace with parasols and potted plants. A regular Prague visitor was unenthusiastic about the *Ada* restaurant (Czech and French fare), but otherwise found much to like: 'Bedrooms luxuriously appointed. Bathrooms superbly fitted. Excellent staff in reception and lounge areas. Breakfast buffet varied and delicious.' Owner/manager Martin Hoffmeister has dedicated his hotel to his father, Adolf – painter, writer and diplomat – whose avant-garde paintings and drawings, including caricatures (James Joyce, Charlie Chaplin, Le Corbusier and others), adorn the walls. There are floral fabrics and chandeliers; the lift is bright and metallic.

Open All year. **Rooms** 10 suites, 23 double, 3 single. **Facilities** Lift. Lobby, bar, wine cellar, café (summer terrace), restaurant. **Location** Near Charles Bridge. **Credit cards** All major cards accepted. **Terms** B&B: single €165–€270, double €200–€310, suite €275–€430; D,B&B €35 added per person.

HOTEL PAŘÍŽ   showpiece

U Obecního Domu 1   *Tel* 00 420 2 22 19 51 95
110 00 Prague 1   *Fax* 00 420 2 24 22 54 75
                                     Email booking@hotel-pariz.cz
                                     Website www.hotel-pariz.cz

This elegant high-towered mansion, built in 1904 in neo-Gothic style near the Old Town Square, is a Prague showpiece. It has an Art Nouveau interior of the 'special Czech variety', full of 'splendid detail' (mosaics, statuettes, wrought-iron fixtures, crystal, all in shades of green, pale blue and gold). Between the wars, the city's café society met here. The Brandejs family owners have renovated and filled it with paintings, and it is now a five-star member of the French group, Concorde. Visitors find it 'delightfully traditional', 'full of charm', and quiet. Bedrooms have much Art Nouveau detail, 'down to the wastepaper baskets', beds are 'luxurious', bathrooms have under-floor heating. The buffet breakfast is 'the best ever', and the service is praised. The hotel's 'sumptuous' *Café de Paris* (with pianist) serves light meals, coffee, cakes and desserts. In the graceful *Sarah Bernhardt* restaurant, chef Radek Pálka's offerings include 'favourite soups of Madam with Camellias', 'Dishes in the style of the mysterious Judith'.

Open All year. **Rooms** 17 suites, 69 deluxe/executive. **Facilities** 1 bar, 2 restaurants; Relax Club with sauna. **Location** Central, 400 m E of Staroměstské náměstí. Parking. **Credit cards** All major cards accepted. **Terms** Room €150–€320, suite €300–€3,700. Breakfast €20. Set lunch €30, dinner €60; full alc €60.

ROMANTIK HOTEL U RAKA   stylish

Černínská 10/93   *Tel* 00 420 2 20 51 11 00
118 00 Prague 1   *Fax* 00 420 2 33 35 80 41
                                   Email uraka@login.cz
                          Website www.romantikhotels.com/prag

Loved for its 'peace and unique style', this stylish little guest house, owned by the 'extremely helpful' Paul family, is up a hill near the castle's north side. 'Its quiet, welcoming atmosphere makes it the perfect place to unwind,' say visitors. In a 'charming spot', in an artists' colony near the castle, the two buildings, on cobbled courtyards, are tasteful imitations of 18th-century barns on this site. The decor is smart and original: tiled floors, open hearths, modern metal and wood furnishings, paintings by local artists for sale. In the kitchen/bar, with its wooden ceiling and open fire, the 'ample' breakfast is served with double damask napkins, 'exquisite' blue and white Czech porcelain. It includes fruit, cereals, yogurts, ham, eggs. Other visitors were impressed by the 'impeccable cleanliness', and the quality of the fittings. The small two-tiered garden 'has an element of the Japanese': snacks can be served here. 'The location can mean a lot of steep walking.'

Open All year. **Rooms** 6 double. **Facilities** Lounge, snack bar/breakfast room. Garden terrace. **Location** Off Loreta Square, 500 m W of castle. Parking. Airport transit arranged. **Restrictions** No smoking during breakfast. **Credit cards** Amex, MasterCard, Visa. **Terms** B&B: single €190–€210, double €210–€230, suite €240–€265.

DENMARK

COPENHAGEN
(easyJet)

The airport is 8 km from the city.

---

71 NYHAVN HOTEL   **prime location**

Nyhavn 71   *Tel* 00 45 33 43 62 00
1051 Copenhagen K   *Fax* 00 45 33 43 62 01
                              Email 71nyhavnhotel@arp-hansen.dk
                       Website www.71nyhavnhotelcopenhagen.dk

A conversion of two old spice warehouses, this hotel is well liked for the service and the location – within walking distance of most of the main sights. It stands among coloured gabled houses at the junction of the Nyhavn canal and the harbour. 'Great hotel; best reception desk in Europe,' says a visitor. Others have praised the 'delightful young staff' and the decor: 'Huge, bright abstract paintings, thick fir beams and posts in public areas and bedrooms. Our medium-sized room had an efficient small shower room, excellent soundproofing.' Sophisticated *Pakhuskælderen* restaurant; a large buffet breakfast. Good weekend rates.

Open All year. Restaurant closed Sun, public holidays. **Rooms** 17 suites, 124 double, 9 single. **Facilities** Lobby/lounge, bar, restaurant. **Location** Central. **Restrictions** No smoking at breakfast. **Credit cards** All major cards accepted. **Terms** Room: single 990–2,350 Dkr, double 1,290–2,350 Dkr, suite 2,190–5,000 Dkr. Breakfast 125 Dkr. Set meals 275–325 Dkr.

ESBJERG
(Ryanair)

The airport is 12 km north of the town.
Ryanair also flies to Aarhus, just over an hour's
drive from these hotels.

SØNDERHO KRO   **luxury**

Kropladsen 11   *Tel* 00 45 75 16 40 09
Sønderho   *Fax* 00 45 75 16 43 85
6720 Fanø   *Email* mail@sonderhokro.dk
                      Website www.sonderhokro.dk

The island of Fanø, just off the coast at Esbjerg, has a 10-mile beach of fine firm sand. In a pretty village near the southern tip, Birgit and Niels Steen Sørensen have built their smart hotel (Relais & Châteaux) in the grounds of one of the oldest inns in Denmark. 'It is very silent here,' they write. Each bedroom is different. 'Ours had exposed beams, a comfortable sofa, a huge thick wooden coffee table, candles,' said a visitor. 'The bathroom, equally large, had the fluffiest towels.' Danish/international dishes are served on a no-choice half-board dinner menu or a short *carte*. Breakfast has freshly baked bread; 'delicious muesli'. Light lunches include local smoked specialities. The 'professional service' is admired.

Open All year, except Christmas, 1 week Jan/Feb. **Rooms** 14 double. **Facilities** Hall, salons, restaurant. Garden. **Location** In SE Sønderho, by church. Ferry from Esbjerg. 12 km to Sønderho. **Credit cards** All major cards accepted. **Terms** Room: single 810–1,100 Dkr, double 1,030–1,420 Dkr; D,B&B 750–1,375 Dkr per person.

STEENSGAARD HERREGÅRDSPENSION
manor house

Steensgaard 4
Millinge
5642 Funen

Tel 00 45 62 61 94 90
Fax 00 45 63 61 78 61
Email steensgaard@herregaardspension.dk
Website www.herregaardspension.dk

Anne Bille-Brahe and Niels Raahauge's 'marvellous' old brick and half-timbered 14th-century moated manor house is on the island of Funen (Fyn), a reasonable drive on the motorway from either Esbjerg or Aarhus airports. 'Fantastic hotel, food, location. A must stay,' says a visitor. It stands in a large park with a lake and a reserve for deer. Public rooms have antiques, portraits, chandeliers, much panelling; hunting trophies are in the hall, and leather-bound volumes in the library. The large candlelit dining room is popular with locals for its modern/French Danish dishes, eg, shrimp soup with asparagus flan; roast lamb marinated with honey, lavender and thyme. The 'attentive service' is praised. The large, light, best bedrooms have windows on several sides; a smaller, cheaper room under the eaves, with its bathroom down the hall, was found 'airy and attractive'. Breakfast is 'the usual Scandinavian buffet, elegantly done'. Good walking in the 'Funen Alps', and on nearby beaches.

Open All year, except 24/25, 31 Dec and 1 Jan. **Rooms** 20 double. 6 in annexe. **Facilities** Hall, 4 lounges, bar, billiard room, restaurant (no-smoking). 2.4 hectare grounds. **Location** NW of Millinge, a village NW of Fåborg. **Credit cards** All major cards accepted. **Terms** B&B: single 905–1,355 Dkr, double 990–1,600 Dkr. Set lunch 195 Dkr, dinner 380 Dkr.

FRANCE

BERGERAC
(FlyBE, Ryanair)

The airport, 5 km south-east of the town, is the gateway to the Dordogne.

HÔTEL DU CENTENAIRE   gourmet

Rocher de la Penne	*Tel* 00 33 5.53.06.68.68
Les Eyzies-de-Tayac	*Fax* 00 33 5.53.06.92.41
24620 Dordogne	*Email* hotel.centenaire@wanadoo.com
	Website www.hotelducentenaire.com

A 'lovely and luxurious' hotel (Relais & Châteaux) beside the river Vézère, just outside Les Eyzies, famous for the discovery of the cave of Cro-Magnon man close by. It is owned by Alain and Geneviève Scholly and chef Roland Mazère, who has two *Michelin* stars for his inventive cuisine, lavish with local truffles, foie gras, cèpes, etc. Decor is modern and sleek. 'The food was excellent but dear,' one visitor wrote. 'Rooms were good value, service was excellent, breakfast a fine buffet.' Many bedrooms are large, with a modern tiled bathroom; some have a balcony overlooking the hills.

Open Early Apr–early Nov. Restaurant closed midday, except Thurs, Sat, Sun and holidays. **Rooms** 5 suites, 14 double. **Facilities** Salon, bar, restaurant; dining terrace; fitness room. Garden: heated swimming pool. **Location** Edge of village. 50 km NE of Bergerac. **Credit cards** All major cards accepted. **Terms** Room €138–€230, suite €260–€381. Breakfast €20. D,B&B €145–€230 per person.

HOSTELLERIE DES DUCS   budget

Boulevard Jean Brissau   *Tel* 00 33 5.53.83.74.58
Duras   *Fax* 00 33 5.53.83.75.03
47120 Lot-et-Garonne   *Email* hostellerie.des.ducs@wanadoo.fr
                            Website www.hostellerieducs-duras.com

Long liked for its 'cordial family atmosphere', the Blanchet family's restaurant-with-rooms, a converted 18th-century convent, is in the centre of this 'delightful' small wine-growing town, some 40 km south-west of Bergerac. Its terrace faces Duras's 14th-century fortress which looks across a vast plain. The bedrooms may be 'nothing special (bathroom with plastic sliding door)', but a returning visitor thought this 'still a very nice place'. The garden is quiet, with a good pool, flowers everywhere. Dining room '*très magnifique*' (with 18th-century decor), but one couple thought it 'dull and dark'. *Gault Millau* has recently raised its score for M. Blanchet's cooking from 13 to 14 points, praising the foie gras de canard à la gousse d'ail; fricassée of local chicken. Previously it has admired Madame's 'smiling welcome'. Other visitors had a room with a small lounge looking over the garden towards vineyards.

Open All year. Restaurant closed Sat midday; also Sun night/Mon Oct–June, Mon midday July–Sept. **Rooms** 13 double, 2 single. **Facilities** Lounge, TV room, billiard room; restaurant; billiard room; terrace (meal service). Garden: swimming pool. **Location** By château. 23 km N of Marmande. **Credit cards** All major cards accepted. **Terms** Room: single €40–€44, double €54–€84. Breakfast €8.50. D,B&B €58–€73 per person.

BIARRITZ
(Ryanair)

The airport is at Anglet, east of Biarritz.

HÔTEL ARCÉ   **rural idyll**

Route du Col d'Ispéguy   *Tel* 00 33 5.59.37.40.14
St-Étienne-de-Baïgorry   *Fax* 00 33 5.59.37.40.27
64430 Pyrénées-Atlantiques *Email* reservations@hotel-arce.com
       Website www.hotel-arce.com

Up the remote Aldudes valley near the Spanish border, the village of St-Étienne-de-Baïgorry is a key Basque folklore centre. Here, Pascal and Christine Arcé's 'beautiful country hotel, idyllically located' by a trout river, is much liked. 'Deeply wonderful: a centre of gourmet cooking which retains the character of a family-run *auberge*.' A family party, aged 18 months to 75, 'was treated with great friendliness'. 'Every detail is lovingly attended to – pleasing room decor, copious breakfasts, enjoyable dinners.' 'On the superb €32 menu, we ate croustillant de légumes; excellent terrine; lamb with garlic purée. Service is friendly, informal. Interesting wines.' 'Our clean, well-furnished room looked over the fast-flowing river': back rooms can be large, but lack a view.

Open Mid-Mar–mid-Nov. Restaurant closed Mon, Wed midday 1 Oct–30 June. **Rooms** 3 suites, 19 double, 1 single. **Facilities** Salon, restaurant. Garden: swimming pool. **Location** 11 km W of St-Jean-Pied-de-Port (35 km SE of Biarritz). Near church. **Credit cards** Diners, MasterCard, Visa. Terms **Room**: single €60–€68, double €109–€130, suite €144–€160. Breakfast €8.50. D,B&B €71–€104 per person.

HÔTEL PARC VICTORIA   luxury

5 rue Cépé
St-Jean-de-Luz
64500 Pyrénées-Atlantiques

Tel 00 33 5.59.26.78.78
Fax 00 33 5.59.26.78.08

Email parcvictoria@relaischateaux.com

Website www.parcvictoria.com

Roger Larralde's 'delightful' hotel (Relais & Châteaux) stands near St-Jean-de-Luz, a popular Basque yachting centre/fishing port 10 km south-west of Biarritz. A regular visitor called it 'the best hotel we have ever stayed in'; another wrote: 'The height of luxury.' But there has been recent criticism, too, of the food (*nouvelle* in quantity') and the service ('poor at breakfast'). Furnished in a mix of Art Nouveau and Art Deco styles, the white, late 19th-century villa stands in 'immaculate' gardens, 'formal and fragrant'. The 'beautiful' pool area 'is the hub of the hotel, lively and fun' – here drinks, lunch and dinner are served. The young chef, Eric Jorge, provides Basque and Landaise cuisine. On dull days, it is served in the formal restaurant with conservatory. 'Staff are delightful, the ambience is truly warm.' 'Our sumptuous room had a terrace with sunshade.' 'Our suite had a private garden, and some very French antiques.' Breakfast, 'a delicious spread', can be taken on the terrace, with pink roses.

Open 15 Mar–15 Nov. Restaurant closed 1 Nov–1 Apr, Tues low season. **Rooms** 8 suites, 8 double. **Facilities** Lounge, bar, 3 dining rooms, conservatory. 1-hectare garden. **Location** From A63 *autoroute*, exit Aix Ouest, go towards hospital Henri Pontier; follow yellow hotel signs. Parking. **Credit cards** All major cards accepted. **Terms** Room €130–€293, suite €243–€342; D,B&B double €242–€383.

BORDEAUX
(bmibaby, FlyBE)

The airport is 30 km west of the city centre.

HAUTERIVE SAINT-JAMES   luxury

3 place Camille Hostein	*Tel* 00 33 5.57.97.06.00
Bouliac	*Fax* 00 33 5.56.20.92.58
Bordeaux	*Email* reception@saintjames-bouilac.com
33270 Gironde	*Website* www.relaischateaux.com/stjames

With a new owner/manager, Jean-Claude Borgel, a new name and a new chef, Michel Portos, this stylish hotel (Relais & Châteaux) is on a hillside in the suburb of Bouliac. A modern complex has been created around a 17th-century farmhouse. It stands in large grounds with vines and a swimming pool. The glass-walled restaurant (*Michelin* star) has a view to the city across the broad Garonne. 'The food is a little different now, but every bit as delicious,' say returning visitors. 'Service as friendly as ever.' Each bedroom, theatrically lit, has a vast bed on a plinth. Summer meals are served on a terrace, and there are two cheaper eateries, the *Bistroy* (fish restaurant) and the *Café de l'Espérance*.

Open All year, except Jan. Main restaurant closed Jan, Sun, Mon. **Rooms** 3 suites, 15 double. **Facilities** Lift. 2 salons, bar, 3 restaurants. **Location** Bouliac, 7 km SE of centre, off Ave G. Cabannes. **Credit cards** All major cards accepted. **Terms** Room: single €137–€168, double €153–€183, suite €231–€267. Breakfast €15. *Café*: alc €25; *Bistroy*: alc €35. Restaurant: set meals €28–€74.

CHÂTEAU CORDEILLAN-BAGES gourmet

Route des Châteaux
Pauillac
33250 Gironde

Tel 00 33 5.56.59.24.24
Fax 00 33 5.56.59.01.89
Email cordeillan@relaischateaux.com
Website www.cordeillanbages.com

The Médoc may be a boring stretch of gravel-based land north-west of Bordeaux, but it produces some of the world's finest red wines. Pauillac is a top *appellation*, and here this 'beautifully decorated' small 17th-century château, now a 'serious hotel with a formal atmosphere' (Relais & Châteaux), stands amid famous vineyards. Its huge wine list has 60 pages devoted to Bordeaux wines. Manager/chef Thierry Marx wins two *Michelin* stars, 17 *Gault Millau* points, eg, for crémeux de concombre semi-pris, caviar de Gironde; agneau de lait en trois façons, served in *nouvelle* portions. 'Expensive, but good value,' was one comment. Other visitors have written: 'Our best meal of the year. Service a good mix of friendly and sophisticated.' There are 'lovely, rather clubby' public rooms, and a charming grassy courtyard where meals are served. Breakfasts and bedrooms are admired. 'Our "superior" room had fine furniture, and a patio with parasols.' Some beds are king-size. 'Superb bath.' Nearby is the Mouton-Rothschild château, with wine museum.

Open 15 Feb–14 Dec. Restaurant closed Sat midday, Tues midday. **Rooms** 4 suites, 25 double. **Facilities** Lift. 3 lounges, breakfast room, restaurant; courtyard, terrace. Garden: heated swimming pool. **Location** 1 km S of Pauillac, 53 km N of Bordeaux. **Restrictions** No smoking: restaurant, some bedrooms. **Credit cards** All major cards accepted. **Terms** Room €132–€270, suite €282–€420. Breakfast €20. Set meals €50–€85.

AU LOGIS DES REMPARTS   charming

18 rue Guadet
St-Émilion
33330 Gironde

Tel 00 33 5.57.24.70.43
Fax 00 33 5.57.74.47.44
Email logis-des-remparts@wanadoo.fr
Website www.saint-emilion.org

The famous vineyards encircle this 'delightful small town', with its medieval houses, steep cobbled traffic-free streets. Now being much enlarged, this B&B hotel is 'a happy, friendly place, run by charming people'. A pale stone building in an old street, it has a lounge 'both comfortable and stylish'. Big bedrooms have modern furniture and a few antiques; some are hung with tapestries. 'Our "suite", with an internal gallery, looked over the handsome breakfast terrace and its olive tree. Breakfast, with fresh orange juice, yogurt, fruit, was delightful. Everything, including the large swimming pool and shady garden (with discreet bar service), was immaculate; the young receptionists were helpful.' On the lawns are tables and chairs under parasols. For meals, *Le Tertre* is liked: 'Superb foie gras de canard; very kind owners.' The owners, M. and Mme Yonnet, also own the *Maison des Templiers*, a historic monument: a conversion is increasing the number of bedrooms to 35, and the garden will also double in size.

Open Mid-Jan–mid-Dec. **Rooms** 19 double. 2 on ground floor. **Facilities** Salon, bar, breakfast conservatory (no-smoking). Garden: terrace, swimming pool. **Location** Main street (rooms soundproofed). Parking (reservation necessary, inaccessible 11 pm–7 am; €10 a night). **Credit cards** MasterCard, Visa. **Terms** Room €68–€150. Breakfast €12.

HÔTEL DES PINS   budget

L'Amélie-sur-Mer   *Tel* 00 33 5.56.73.27.27
33780 Gironde   *Fax* 00 33 5.56.73.60.39
                                 Email hotel.pin@wanadoo.fr
                                 Website www.hotel-des-pins.com

On the Atlantic coast, near the tip of the Médoc peninsula, 'Soulac is a proper little seaside town of real character', and l'Amélie is a 'sort of suburb'. Here, this spruce Logis de France, white-fronted, red-roofed, is much admired: 'M. and Mme Moulin keep their eye on their very well-run hotel, he at reception, she in the dining room and the hotel generally. They have a fine sense of humour and an excellent staff. At breakfast each day we received the *demi-pension* dinner menu, with a request to tell Monsieur by 10 am if any dish did not meet our wishes. On two occasions, we asked for an alternative and this was readily agreed. The menu was never repeated. The restaurant was always full, but residents were not given short shrift. Large wine list.' An earlier visitor 'was impressed by the welcome, the family feel, the excellent value and the breakfast'. The garden has a wide lawn, pine trees, deckchairs and parasols. Close by is a vast sandy beach.

Open 20 Mar–1 Nov. Closed Sat midday, Sun/Mon Oct–May. **Rooms** 31. **Facilities** Salon, restaurant. Garden (outdoor dining). **Location** 5 km SW of Soulac-sur-Mer. 99 km NW of Bordeaux. Frequent ferries from Royan. **Credit cards** All major cards accepted. **Terms** Room €40–€80. Breakfast €6.50–€7.50. D,B&B (obligatory 31 July–24 Aug) €41–€66 per person.

BREST
(Ryanair)

The airport is 10 minutes' drive
inland from the port city.

HÔTEL LA BAIE DES ANGES   *chic*

350 route des Anges   *Tel* 00 33 2.98.04.90.04
Port de l'Aber Wrac'h   *Fax* 00 33 2.98.04.92.27
Landéda   *Email* contact@baie-des-anges.com
29870 Finistère   *Website* www.baie-des-anges.com

On the Pays des Abers coast, north of Brest, this new B&B
hotel (Relais du Silence), painted yellow, is run by its owners,
France Barre and her partner, Jacques Briant. 'A very good
team: he is an absolute charmer,' says the visitor who
discovered it. 'The location is smashing, on the eponymous
bay. Cool, chic seaside decor (wicker and carefully chosen
objets). Delightful bedrooms, most with sea view. Fabulous
breakfast.' Most rooms are spacious. The annexe, *La Marine*,
has six studios, each accommodating up to three people.
Plenty of restaurants at the port, a few minutes' walk away.

Open All year, except 3 Jan–15 Feb. **Rooms** 2 suites, 24 double.
Facilities Salon/bar, breakfast room; sauna, hydromassage.
Location 25 km N of Brest. Parking. **Restriction** Smoking in bar
only. **Credit cards** MasterCard, Visa. **Terms** Room €68–€135,
suite €154–€174. Breakfast €12–€14.

HÔTEL DE LA PLAGE   favourite

À la plage   *Tel* 00 33 2.98.92.50.12
Ste-Anne-la-Palud   *Fax* 00 33 2.98.92.56.54
29550 Finistère   *Email* laplage@relaischateaux.com
                       Website www.relaischateaux.com/laplage

Secluded on a huge sandy beach near the old fishing port of
Douarnenez, south of Brest, this 'lovely hotel' (Relais &
Châteaux) is an old favourite, run 'with panache' by its
owners, Anne and Jean Milliau Le Coz. It has unusually good
food (*Michelin* star for Hervé Pachoud) for a seaside holiday
hotel. The spectacular tiered conservatory dining room is
for residents; the older dining room, with Venetian crystal
chandeliers, is for locals. 'Dinner was excellent,' says a
visitor. Others have written: 'The young staff, in black and
white uniforms, are friendly; cooking is robust and good.
Delectable sorbets; excellent wines. Public rooms are quite
smart; the spacious bar has sea views from comfy sofas.'
'Our room had bags of seaside character.' 'There were many
families with children.' Breakfast is a buffet. Many bedrooms
face the sea; some are spacious; some have period Breton
furniture. The gardens are 'immaculate', and the swimming
pool is useful at low tide when the sea goes far out (the rapid
incoming tide makes caution necessary).

Open 1 Apr–10 Nov. Restaurant closed midday on Tues, Wed
and Fri. **Rooms** 4 suites, 26 double. 6 in annexe, 50 m. **Facilities**
Lift. 2 salons, games room, bar, restaurant; sauna. **Location** On
coast, W of Plonevez-Porzay by D61. Car park. **Credit cards** All
major cards accepted. **Terms** Room €85–€264, suite €232–€264.
Breakfast €14.50. D,B&B double €275–€386.

LE BRITTANY   seaside style

Boulevard Sainte-Barbe	*Tel* 00 33 2.98.69.70.78
BP 47	*Fax* 00 33 2.98.61.13.29
Roscoff	*Email* hotel.brittany@wanadoo.fr
29681 Finistère	*Website* www.hotel-brittany.com

In a pleasant Brittany harbour town, this solid granite 17th-century house faces a sandy beach, just east of the port and centre. It is now a stylish hotel with a 'welcoming owner', Mme Chapalain. The sea-facing restaurant, *Le Yachtman*, with its huge fireplace, serves Loïc Le Bail's *'cuisine du terroir'* (eg, salpicon de chair d'araignée; tartare de langoustines). 'Delicious food, especially the puddings.' There is a terrace by the sea for summer meals. The best bedrooms, with views of sea or town, are in the main house. 'Ours, white and spacious, had four windows with long yellow curtains: one opened on to a private terrace with loungers. Stylish bathroom.' The rooms in the modern extension by the covered swimming pool are not much liked. Breakfast includes fresh pastries, orange juice, yogurt, and is mostly enjoyed. The car-free Île de Batz, opposite, is worth visiting.

Open 25 Mar–21 Oct. Restaurant closed midday. **Rooms** 2 suites, 23 double. 6 in extension. **Facilities** Lift. Lounge/bar, breakfast room, restaurant; meeting room. Garden: café. **Location** Near ferry terminal, 2 km E of centre. Parking. **Credit cards** Amex, MasterCard, Visa. **Terms** Room €90–€140, suite €160–€206. Breakfast €12. D,B&B double €192–€260. Set dinner €26–€53.

CARCASSONNE
(Ryanair)

The airport is 3 km from Carcassonne.
Ryanair promotes it as an entry point for
Toulouse, 91 km away.

LA BASTIDE DE CABEZAC   à la mode

18–20 Hameau de Cabezac	*Tel* 00 33 4.68.46.66.10
Bize-Minervois	*Fax* 00 33 4.68.46.66.29
11120 Aude	*Email* bastidecabezac@aol.com
	Website www.labastidecabezac.com

Set among Minervois vineyards some 40 km north-east of
Carcassonne, this 18th-century *relais de poste*, 'reasonably
priced, stylish, very French', is run by its owners, Sabine and
Hervé dos Santos. 'They are charming, thoughtful hosts,'
says a visitor. 'He cooks fresh seasonal food with a light
touch; breakfast has fresh juice and yogurt.' Meals are served
in an airy restaurant, or outdoors. 'The style is pale
distressed wood, lavender, coir matting, white linen; all clean
and fragrant. Staff attentive but not overbearing. Despite the
proximity of a busy road, we were not bothered by traffic
noise. In the heat of August we were grateful for the clean,
adequately sized swimming pool, and the air-conditioning in
our bedroom.'

Open All year. Restaurant closed Sat midday, Sun night/Mon
Sept–Apr. **Rooms** 2 suites, 12 double. **Facilities** Restaurant.
Patio. Garden. **Location** 20 km NW of Narbonne, 3 km S of Bize-
Minervois on D5. **Credit cards** Probably some accepted. **Terms**
Double room €69–€115. Breakfast €10. Set meals €23–€39.

DOMAINE D'AURIAC   classical

Route de St-Hilaire   *Tel* 00 33 4.68.25.72.22
11009 Carcassonne   *Fax* 00 33 4.68.47.35.54
                              Email auriac@relaischateaux.com
                          Website www.relaischateaux.com/auriac

Outside Carcassonne, this luxurious hotel (Relais & Châteaux) is a handsome 19th-century mansion in classical style. Set in its own park, with an 18-hole golf course, it is just across the motorway (out of earshot) from the hilltop fortress. 'The pool and grounds are very attractive, and the food is very good,' says a visitor. Most bedrooms are traditionally furnished and large, but some are small, their bathrooms too. Some are in buildings in the grounds. 'Our room, light and airy, opened on to balconies facing the garden.' Another couple had an 'enormous and handsome room, with a cupboard but no drawers: we had to keep half our clothes in our suitcase'. Owner/chef Bernard Rigaudis (his wife, Anne-Marie, is manager) has a *Michelin* star. Fires blaze in winter in the spacious public rooms. One couple thought there was 'a lack of charm about the place', but others wrote of 'friendly staff', an 'elegant, but unostentatious' atmosphere. Breakfast on the terrace is 'delightful'.

Open All year, except 4 Jan–9 Feb, 27 Apr–5 May, 16–24 Nov, Sun night/Mon Oct–Apr. **Rooms** 26 double. **Facilities** Lift, ramps. 4 salons, 2 bars, restaurant. Terrace. **Location** 2.5 km SE of town. From A61 exit Carcassonne Ouest; then go in direction of Centre Hospitalier. **Credit cards** All major cards accepted. **Terms** Room €100–€420. Breakfast €19. D,B&B €80 added per person. Set meals €47–€100.

LA FERME DE LA SAUZETTE   tranquil

Route de Villefloure   *Tel* 00 33 4.68.79.81.32
Palaja   *Fax* 00 33 4.68.79.65.99
Cazilhac   *Email* info@lasauzette.com
11570 Aude   *Website* www.lasauzette.com

Just south of Carcassonne, this *chambres d'hôtes* is 'a haven of rural tranquillity'. 'Very good for children,' says a visitor. The owners, Chris and Diana Gibson, are 'delightful hosts'. Their former farmhouse stands amid Corbières vineyards, and within easy driving distance of the wild Cathar country further south. Two granaries, with original exposed beams, have been turned into five bedrooms and a large living/dining room. 'The decor is earthily artistic, the bedrooms are pretty and rustic, and their lighting is very good.' The all-inclusive no-choice dinner, 'a bargain', is communally served (alfresco in fine weather) round a large table, after an aperitif at 8 pm. 'A fine fish and spinach pie; local sheep and goat cheeses; one night some French regulars turned up with buckets of juicy oysters.' Other visitors wrote: 'We loved it. Breakfast (with fresh breads, home-made jams, local honey, yogurt) was delicious; dinner was convivial.' The spacious lounge has an open fire. A cat, and the teenage Gibson children, are often around.

Open Feb–Oct, Dec. **Rooms** 5 double. **Facilities** Living/dining room. Veranda, terrace. 2-hectare garden. **Location** S of Cazilhac on Villefloure road; 5 km S of Carcassonne. Parking. **Restrictions** No smoking: bedrooms; at table. **Credit cards** None accepted. **Terms** (Min. 2 nights May–Sept) B&B: single €53–€63, double €60–€70; D,B&B €57– €90 per person. Set dinner (with wine and coffee) €27.

CHÂTEAU DE FLOURE   welcoming

1 allée Gaston Bonheur
Floure
11800 Aude

Tel 00 33 4.68.79.11.29
Fax 00 33 4.68.79.04.61
Email contact@chateau-de-floure.com
Website www.chateau-de-floure.com

In a small village near Carcassonne, at the foot of Mount Alaric, this handsome creeper-girt mansion has been converted from a Romanesque abbey, part 12th-century. It stands in a park with vineyards, formal gardens, and a large swimming pool, 'sometimes full of children'. Recent visitors called it 'a delightful place, of shabby charm', with 'excellent food, friendly service'. Others have written of 'delightful public rooms, accommodating staff, very good dinners'. The owners, Jorry and Dominique Assous, are 'warmly welcoming'; he is 'jovial'. They have made many improvements: a 'Victorian' veranda with a bar; a breakfast room, a lift; near the pool, an outdoor lunch brasserie with grills and salads. Robert Rodriguez cooks 'fantastic five-course feasts', served in a courtyard in summer. The public rooms are filled with *objets d'art*. The lounge has huge old murals; a grand piano adorns the bar. The continental breakfast is 'standard', but an American variety is offered. 'One bedroom was spacious, with a balcony and French country furniture; the other was more modern, less charming.'

Open 23 Mar–31 Oct. Restaurant closed Mon and Wed midday. **Rooms** 5 suites, 11 double. **Facilities** Lift. Salon, bar, restaurant. **Location** Outside village. 9 km E of Carcassonne, off N113. **Credit cards** All major cards accepted. **Terms** Room €100–€170, suite €230. Breakfast €16. D,B&B €47 added per person.

CHAMBÉRY
(FlyBE)

The airport, 8 km outside the city, is a good
springboard for a summer Alpine break.

LA TOUR DE PACORET   budget

Montailleur	*Tel* 00 33 4.79.37.91.59
Grésy-sur-Isère	*Fax* 00 33 4.79.37.93.84
73460 Savoie	*Email* info@hotel-pacoret-savoie.com
	Website www.hotel-pacoret-savoie.com

'The best place I've stayed in; excellent value,' wrote an
enthusiast of this fairly modest but 'unusual' and 'romantic'
hotel/restaurant (Relais du Silence). It stands above the Isère
valley outside this 'tiny, quaint' Alpine village near Albertville
(some 50 km from Chambéry). Owned and run by Gilles and
Laurence Chardonnet ('their staff could not be more friendly'),
it is a 'beautiful stone tower' with modern extensions. 'Our
lovely room had restored antiques and rich tapestries.
Excellent food and service. Delicious breakfast pastries.' A
potager supplies the kitchen, and some dishes are Savoyard.
The dining room has wide views, and a wisteria-shaded terrace.
In the garden is a swimming pool with loungers. In winter the
Chardonnets run the *Hôtel Alba* in Méribel.

Open Early May–end Oct. Restaurant closed Wed midday except
July/Aug, Tues midday except Aug. **Rooms** 8 double, 2 single.
Facilities Salon, restaurant. Garden. **Location** 1.5 km NE of Grésy,
12 km SW of Albertville. Parking. **Credit cards** MasterCard, Visa.
Terms B&B: single €55, double €64–€94; D,B&B €60–€75 per
person.

HÔTEL BEAU SITE   lakeside

Rue André Thuriet	*Tel* 00 33 4.50.60.71.04
Talloires	*Fax* 00 33 4.50.60.79.22
74290 Haute-Savoie	*Email* hotelbeausite@free.fr
	Website www.hotel-beausite-fr.com

The lawns (with loungers, plenty of space for sunbathing) reach down to glorious Lake Annecy, in the large garden of this handsome white 1895 villa. Long admired, it is run by Anne Conan, daughter of the founder, Louis, with a long-serving staff, including Patrick Durand as chef. Regular visitors have written: 'Three very enjoyable dinners: set menus less sophisticated than the *à la carte*, but excellent value – delicious féra fresh from the lake; crème brûlée the size of a small skating rink.' 'Breakfast, in the garden, was lovely.' 'Our small first-floor room had a tiny bathroom and a loo in a cupboard, but a large balcony with a gorgeous view of the lake and the mountains.' Some rooms are large. The decor is modern; the salon, in a cosy red, has attractive pictures; the spacious dining room is 'Italianate in feel'. Guests on B&B terms tend to stay in the annexe, *La Tournette*.

Open 10 May–10 Oct. **Rooms** 1 suite, 27 double, 1 single. **Facilities** Lounge, lounge/bar, breakfast room, restaurant. 1-hectare garden. **Location** Village centre: E side of lake. 12 km S of Annecy (40 km NE of Chambéry). Parking. **Restrictions** No smoking: breakfast room, bedrooms. **Credit cards** All major cards accepted. **Terms** Room: single €63–€65, double €77–€142, suite €134–€180. Breakfast €12. D,B&B €75–€126 per person.

DINARD
(Ryanair)

The airport is in the suburbs of Dinard.

HÔTEL DES DUNES   budget

Rue Primauguet   *Tel* 00 33 2.96.41.80.31
St-Cast-le-Guildo   *Fax* 00 33 2.96.41.85.34
22380 Côtes-d'Armor

'A real find.' In a lively resort 20 km from Dinard, this large stone building is a pleasant holiday hotel, owned and run by brothers Jacques and Pierre Féret ('excellent cooks') and their wives. Visitors (five adults and two children) had a 'wonderful' stay: 'Everyone was very friendly, and particularly helpful about the children's food. Our meals, on *demi-pension*, were outstanding, with a big choice, and oysters and/or shellfish daily.' One couple, on their sixth visit, wrote: 'The dining room is pristine, menus are fairly priced and carefully executed. Standards of housekeeping are high.' The position is 'perfect for the beach'. Bedrooms tend to be on the small side: the best ones, some with a deep balcony, face the gardens and tennis court.

Open 26 Apr–30 Sept. **Rooms** 27. **Facilities** Lounge, bar, restaurant. Garden: tennis. **Location** 20 km W of Dinard. Parking. **Credit cards** MasterCard, Visa. **Terms** Room €49–€65. Breakfast €7.50. D,B&B €62–€66 per person. Set meals €19–€64.

HÔTEL L'ÉCRIN ET RESTAURANT
JEAN-PIERRE CROUZIL
creative cuisine

20 les quais
Plancoët
22130 Côtes-d'Armor

Tel 00 33 2.96.84.10.24
Fax 00 33 2.96.84.01.93
Email jean-pierre.crouzil@wanadoo.fr
Website www.crouzil.com

'Exceptional. It has vitality, panache, and a warmth we have met nowhere else,' say devotees of this remarkable restaurant-with-rooms in a village west of Dinan. Renowned for his creative cooking of local fresh fish, owner/chef Jean-Pierre Crouzil wins two *Michelin* stars, 16 *Gault Millau* points. 'Equally delightful' is his wife, Collette, who fronts and has produced the 'interesting paintings' in the 'striking' dining room, which has 'dazzlingly lit glassed alcoves displaying attractive china, exquisite flower arrangements, elegant glasses and cutlery'. 'Superbly presented food, delicious beyond belief. Monsieur comes out of the kitchen to offer suggestions. On half board you can take any menu. Service was swift and personal. Bags of character.' *L'Écrin* is on a busy main road next to the station car park and opposite the post office. Behind a modest exterior is 'Ali Baba's cave – bronzes, marble staircase, quality fabrics and carpets, luxurious plants. Our big bedroom had a splendid antique chest, smart lamps, spacious bathroom. Breakfast has fresh pastries, delicious home-made jams.'

Open All year, except holidays in Jan, evenings of 25 Dec, 1 Jan. **Rooms** 1 suite, 6 double. **Facilities** Salon, restaurant; sauna, solarium. **Location** Main road, by station. 15 km SW of Dinard. **Credit cards** Amex, MasterCard, Visa. **Terms** Room: single €75, double €105, suite €160. Breakfast €14–€23. D,B&B (min. 3 days) €130–€145 per person.

LE VALMARIN   elegant

7 rue Jean XXIII, St-Servan
St-Malo
35400 Ille-et-Vilaine

Tel 00 33 2.99.81.94.76
Fax 00 33 2.99.81.30.03
Email levalmarin@wanadoo.fr
Website www.levalmarin.com

St-Malo is an attractive old port across the bay from Dinard, too often overlooked by those arriving or leaving on a ferry (not a problem when you take a budget flight). Françoise and Gérard Nicolas's 18th-century house, elegantly renovated in period style, 'quiet and relaxing', stands in a small park near the beach in St-Servan, south of the old town. Returning visitors write: 'Flawless presentation, a superb breakfast.' Others wrote: 'Our lovely high-ceilinged room overlooked the enchanting garden.' The bedrooms have antique furniture; some are up steps (no lift); the spacious ones on the first floor are particularly liked. Breakfast can be served in the garden on fine days: it includes cake, fruit, 'first-class croissants'. No restaurant. *L'Atre*, near the port, serves 'excellent fish'. *La Corderie*, inexpensive, is enjoyed for its good food, its art show and sea view.

Open All year. **Rooms** 12 double. **Facilities** Reception, bar/tea room, breakfast room. Garden. **Location** In St-Servan, 200 m from sea. 2 km S of old St-Malo. Car park. **Credit cards** Amex, MasterCard, Visa. **Terms** Room €95–€135. Breakfast €10.

MAISONS DE BRICOURT   gourmet

---

1 rue Duguesclin	*Tel* 00 33 2.99.89.64.76
Cancale	*Fax* 00 33 2.99.89.88.47
35260 Ille-et-Vilaine	*Email* bricourt@relaischateaux.com
	Website www.maisons-de-bricourt.com

'Extreme comfort, superb food and great views' are offered by owner/chef Olivier Roellinger and his wife, Jane, in their collection of *maisons* (Relais & Châteaux) in and around this picturesque fishing port renowned for its oysters. The famous *Relais Gourmand O Roellinger* (two *Michelin* stars, 19 *Gault Millau* points), in Cancale, has been converted from Roellinger's childhood home. Here, recent guests enjoyed dinner: 'A grand affair, but without pomposity: the ten-course *dégustation* menu was a stunning sequence of flavours, subtly spiced. Super service.' There are five 'rustic' bedrooms in *Les Rimains* in Cancale: 'Its small garden with chairs extends to the cliff-top.' *Château Richeux*, 'a lovely little 1920s villa', is in a lush park, at St-Méloir-des-Ondes, six kilometres away. It has its own *bistrot marin, Le Coquillage*. Here, say recent guests, 'our room, Anise Étoilée, was superb, mosaics around the walls, a lovely bathroom tiled to match. Art Deco furniture, super bed, CD-player, stunning sunrise view across to Mont-St-Michel.'

Open *Les Rimains* mid-Mar–mid-Dec; *Richeux* all year; *Relais* closed Mon midday, Fri midday, Tues, Wed except evenings July/Aug. *Coquillage* closed midday on Mon, Tues and Fri. **Rooms** *Rimains* 5, *Richeux* 13. **Facilities** Lift. Salon, 2 restaurants. 3-hectare garden. **Credit cards** All major cards accepted. **Terms** Room: *Rimains* €145–€230, *Richeux* €160–€290, suite from €300. Breakfast €16. *Relais:* set lunch €86, dinner €145; alc €100–€140. *Coquillage:* set meals €26–€44.

LIMOGES
(FlyBE, Ryanair)

The airport is 12 km north-west of the town.

LA CHAPELLE SAINT-MARTIN   comfort

Nieul-près-Limoges   *Tel* 00 33 5.55.75.80.17
87510 Haute-Vienne   *Fax* 00 33 5.55.75.89.50
                   Email chapelle@relaischateaux.com
                   Website www.chapellesaintmartin.com

'Not easy to find' (it is north-west of Limoges, near Nieul), this *gentilhommière* (Relais & Châteaux) stands in a large park. The large grey house is 'not impressive from the road', but its 'calm comfort' was enjoyed by a visitor. 'It is something special, small, with beautifully furnished, very comfortable bedrooms; one feels one is staying in a private house. Service and food very enjoyable.' Chef/*patron*, Gilles Dudognon, has a *Michelin* star for dishes like œufs vapeur aux truffes; veal with cannelloni of beetroot. At the rear, a modern conservatory faces the extensive lawns and forests of the estate, and there is a swimming pool. All bedrooms have just been renovated: new tapestries, paintings, carpets, etc.

Open 1 Feb–end Dec. Restaurant closed Mon, Tues/Wed midday. **Rooms** 3 suites, 7 double. **Facilities** Bar, restaurant; terrace. 40-hectare park. **Location** S of Nieul. 10 km NW of Limoges by N141 towards Angoulême. **Credit cards** All major cards accepted. **Terms** Room €105–€198, suite €229; D,B&B €115–€183 per person.

AU MOULIN DE LA GORCE   elegance

St-Yrieix-la-Perche
La Roche-L'Abeille
87800 Haute-Vienne

Tel 00 33 5.55.00.70.66
Fax 00 33 5.55.00.76.57
Email moulindelagorce@wanadoo.fr
Website www.moulindelagorce.com

Deep in wooded Limousin countryside, Pierre and Isabelle Bertranet's 16th-century mill house stands enchantingly by a big pond with ducks and a stream, surrounded by old trees. It is now an elegant small hotel (Relais & Châteaux), long adored by visitors ('an oasis of calm'), where guests enjoy M. Bertranet's 'superb food, beautifully served', in the galleried dining room or outdoors (*Michelin* star, 16 *Gault Millau* points for, eg, frogs' legs with millefeuille of avocado; veau de lait au vin jaune). 'At breakfast, by the pond, ducks and carp competed for our crumbs.' Staff are 'efficient and courteous'. The bedrooms, named after flowers, are in the main house and the mill ('the sound of the mill race lulls one to sleep'); some have old beams, some, reached up twisty stairs, are small. Their decor (expensive fabrics, bright colours, antiques and bibelots) 'is more château than mill', one guest said. Nearby are the two porcelain centres of Limoges (large and ugly) and St-Yrieix (small and lovely).

Open 2 Apr–1 Dec. Restaurant closed Mon/Tues/Wed midday. **Rooms** 1 suite (in garden), 9 double; 3 in main building, 6 in mill. **Facilities** Salon, 2 dining rooms. Garden. **Location** 2 km S of La Roche, off D17, 12 km NE of St-Yrieix, off D704. **Credit cards** All major cards accepted. **Terms** Room €68–€150, suite €206. Breakfast €13. D,B&B €105–€174 per person.

HOSTELLERIE LE GRAND ST-LÉONARD   gourmet

23 avenue du Champs de Mars   *Tel* 00 33 5.55.56.18.18
St-Léonard-de-Noblat   *Fax* 00 33 5.55.56.98.32
87400 Haute-Vienne   *Email* grandsaintleonard@wanadoo.fr

East of Limoges, in a charming little medieval hilltop town with a 'fantastic' church (part 11th-century), this large, white, former coaching inn is run by owner/chef Jean-Marc Vallet, 'very helpful and jolly'. In the big, beamed restaurant, with shining copperware and Limoges porcelain, he has a *Michelin* star for his *cuisine classique*: specialities include terrine de foie de canard au Sauternes; croustillant de langoustines aux girolles. 'Excellent food, good value. A budget room,' says a recent visitor. An earlier guest wrote: 'Our bedroom (No. 1) was excellent, with a good bathroom. Not a great view, but fun for one night as we could overhear the cooks and waitresses chatting.'

Open All year, except 12–19 May, 22 Dec–26 Jan, Tues midday, Mon except evenings 15 June–15 Sept. **Rooms** 13 double. **Facilities** Lounge, restaurant. **Location** Edge of town. 21 km E of Limoges. **Credit cards** All major cards accepted. **Terms** Room €52–€57. Breakfast €9. D,B&B €74 per person.

LYON
(easyJet, Ryanair to St-Étienne)

Lyon airport is 25 km east of the city.
St-Étienne is 60 km south-west.

HÔTEL DES ARTISTES   value

---

8 rue Gaspard-André   *Tel* 00 33 4.78.42.04.88
69002 Lyon   *Fax* 00 33 4.78.42.93.76
                              Email hartiste@club-internet.fr

'Friendly, unpretentious, very central', this B&B hotel, by the Théâtre des Célestins, is used by many visiting actors, hence the *artistes* of its name. 'The bedrooms are small but nicely decorated,' says a recent guest: they are modern, bright, double-glazed. 'All is well looked after.' A Cocteau-style mural is in the breakfast room. A good choice if you want to concentrate your resources on eating out in the gastronomic capital of France.

Open All year. **Rooms** 45. **Facilities** Lift. Lounge, bar, breakfast room. **Location** Central, near Place Bellecour. **Credit cards** All major cards accepted. **Terms** Room: single €69–€97, double €75–€103. Breakfast €8.50.

COUR DES LOGES   contemporary

6 rue du Boeuf   *Tel* 00 33 4.72.77.44.44
69005 Lyon   *Fax* 00 33 4.72.40.93.61
                                  Email contact@courdesloges.com
                                  Website www.courdesloges.com

In the trendy St-Jean quarter of Vieux Lyon, four adjacent Renaissance mansions have been converted by Jocelyne and Jean-Louis Sibuet to give a 'breathtakingly contemporary interior, a triumph of design over function', says a visitor. 'There are lovely gardens scattered behind at all levels, and many can be entered directly from the rooms.' Other guests 'were delighted by the setting in lively narrow streets' and 'loved the magnificent atrium, with its dark red cloisters and stunning modern paintings, the helpful concierges, the comfort of the rooms, the minimalist elegance'. It can take time to learn to operate the high-tech fittings in bedrooms and bathrooms, and one couple thought the building 'elegant and charming', but found their room too hot. The restaurant wins a *Michelin* star, 18 *Gault Millau* points (book well ahead), and there are plenty of other restaurants nearby. Breakfast is 'outstanding and varied' (ham on the bone; smoked salmon, etc). There is a roof garden, a wine cellar (tastings are held), and a small mosaic-tiled swimming pool.

Open All year. **Rooms** 10 suites, 37 double, 15 single. **Facilities** Lifts. Lobby, atrium, bar, restaurant. Terraces/hanging garden. **Location** Vieux Lyon, 1 km NW of main station. **Credit cards** All major cards accepted. **Terms** Room: single €220, double €245, suite €420. Breakfast €22. Set meals €60–€110; full alc €90.

MARSEILLE
(easyJet, Thomsonfly)

The airport is 25 km north-west of Marseille.

LE PETIT NICE   exclusive

Le Petit Nice – Passédat	*Tel* 00 33 4.91.59.25.92
Anse de Maldormé	*Fax* 00 33 4.91.59.28.08
Corniche Kennedy	*Email* passedat@relaischateaux.com
13007 Marseille	*Website* www.petitnice-passedat.com

Marseille's most exclusive little hotel (Relais & Châteaux) stands on a rocky corniche by the sea, just south of the port. It consists of several buildings down alleyways. The bedrooms, in two villas, are contemporary. The best have a terrace; all have a sea view. The restaurant, a Hellenic-style villa, has a pretty garden and a picture window looking across the bay. You can dine on the terrace by the outdoor sea-water *piscine*. *Michelin* awards two stars, *Gault Millau* 16 points, for the inventive fish dishes of Gérald Passédat, the third generation of the family which has owned the hotel since it was built in 1917. Breakfast includes 'delicious home-made jams'. 'Because of security, things are a bit Fort Knox-like.'

Open All year. Restaurant closed Sun/Mon low season. **Rooms** 3 suites, 13 double. **Facilities** Lift, ramps. Salon, bar, restaurant. Garden. **Location** 4 km SW of centre, off Corniche Kennedy, follow signs for Vieux Port, Le Pharo. **Credit cards** All major cards accepted. **Terms** Room €190–€450, junior suite €390–€490, suite €610–€790. Breakfast €25. D,B&B €140 added per person.

RELAIS DE LA MAGDELEINE   bastide chic

Rond-point de la Fontaine	*Tel* 00 33 4.42.32.20.16
Gémenos	*Fax* 00 33 4.42.32.02.26
13420 Bouches-du-Rhône	*Email* contact@relais-magdeleine.com
	Website www.relais-magdeleine.com

'Delightful all round.' 'The nicest hotel we know.' 'A charming welcome.' The Marignane brothers' 'beautiful old *bastide*', 40 minutes' drive from Marseille airport, is outside a small town below the mountains of the Massif de la Sainte Baume. It stands in a large walled garden with a lovely swimming pool and a friendly donkey. A recent visitor loved the decor: 'Sort of *Elle* shabby chic meets rustic Louis XV. Everything of the highest standard. It runs smooth as clockwork. No pretension. Staff are helpful but in the background, exactly as it should be.' Magnificent plane trees shade the terrace: at one end are sofas where drinks are served to Schubert or Mozart. You dine at the other end, or in the 'superb' restaurant: 'Philippe is the accomplished chef; Christophe and Vincent manage, with efficiency and multilingual charm.' Their mother is still 'very much around'. 'The bedrooms are beautifully furnished. Prices are reasonable.' 'Most elegant. Great peace and quiet.'

Open 15 Mar–1 Dec. Restaurant closed Mon midday. **Rooms** 2 suites, 20 double, 2 single. **Facilities** Lift, ramps. 2 lounges, 2 dining rooms. **Location** Outskirts of Gémenos. 23 km E of Marseille, 10 km NE of Cassis. A52 exit Pont de l'Étoile. **Credit cards** All major cards accepted. **Terms** Room: single €80–€120, double €95–€185, suite €190–€215. Breakfast €13. D,B&B €98–€170 per person.

HÔTEL ST-CHRISTOPHE   budget

2 avenue Victor-Hugo   *Tel* 00 33 4.42.26.01.24
13100 Aix-en-Provence   *Fax* 00 33 4.42.38.53.17
                    Email saintchristophe@francemarket.com
                    Website www.hotel-saintchristophe.com

Very central, near the Cours Mirabeau, the Bonnets' 'very friendly family hotel', decorated in Art Deco style, has been repeatedly enjoyed by guests. 'Wonderful.' 'Excellent value.' 'The food was not brilliant, but the New Year celebrations were such fun.' 'The breakfast buffet has lots of choice. Bedrooms can be smallish, but the furnishings are excellent; and the *insonorisation* means there is almost no traffic noise.' Best rooms have a terrace. The hotel's *Brasserie Léopold*, hung with pictures painted for it in 1936 by a local artist, Marcel Arnaud, serves many varieties of sauerkraut ('de la mer', Alsacienne, etc). Its bar provides teas, ice creams and 'colourful cocktails'.

Open All year. **Rooms** 7 suites, 51 double. **Facilities** Lift. Restaurant, breakfast room. **Location** Central, near W end of Cours Mirabeau. Private parking (reserve). Garage €9.50. **Credit cards** All major cards accepted. **Terms** Room: single €67–€100, double €73–€109. Breakfast €8.50.

LE PIGONNET   Provençal

5 avenue du Pigonnet   *Tel* 00 33 4.42.59.02.90
13090 Aix-en-Provence   *Fax* 00 33 4.42.59.47.77
Email reservation@hotelpigonnet.com
Website www.hotelpigonnet.com

Cézanne sometimes painted Mont Ste-Victoire from the lovely garden of this 19th-century mansion; today some bedrooms have a balcony with views of it. In a dullish district south of Aix's historic centre, it is now a sophisticated hotel decorated in Provençal style, owned and run since 1924 by the Swellen family, who 'take a personal interest in their guests'. 'Excellent staff. The delightful garden and pool make the walk into the town worthwhile,' runs recent praise. There are rose bowers, fountains and ornamental ponds, and a terrace with a heated swimming pool surrounded by loungers. The dining room is attractive, with much yellow, and dining on hot nights under chestnut trees on a terrace is enjoyed. One guest liked her 'pretty room': most bedrooms have antiques and cheerful fabrics, but one was thought 'dull and shabby' by a dissenter. Some traffic noise, and a recent visitor worried about 'an increasing number of tacky shops' in the neighbourhood.

Open All year. Restaurant closed Sat/Sun midday Nov–end Mar; Sat midday and Sun midday Apr–end Oct. **Rooms** 1 suite, 49 double. **Facilities** 2 lifts. 2 lounges, bar, TV room, restaurant with terrace. **Location** 1 km SW of centre. From motorway: Pont de l'Arc exit towards centre; 3rd traffic light on left. **Credit cards** All major cards accepted. **Terms** Room: single €130–€300, double €160–€350, suite €450–€500. Breakfast €15–€25. D,B&B €56 added per person.

MONTPELLIER
(Ryanair)

The airport is 8 km east of the town.

HÔTEL LE GUILHEM   value

18 rue Jean-Jacques Rousseau	*Tel* 00 33 4.67.52.90.90
Montpellier	*Fax* 00 33 4.67.60.67.67
34000 Hérault	*Email* hotel-le-guilhem@mnet.fr
	Website www.leguilhem.com

Once a sleepy wine centre, Montpellier now has some grandiose modern architecture. But it is full of historical interest too, and has a charming *vieille ville*, well restored. Here, down a narrow street, this group of fine 16th/17th-century buildings is now an appealing **B&B** hotel. The owner, Eric Charpentier, has made many changes recently: 'New reception, a second lift, new rooms.' 'Strong support' came from visitors: 'Our annexe room at the back, overlooking the cathedral [its bells are silent at night], was comfortable, quiet, well maintained. Spacious bathroom with piping hot water. Good continental breakfast': it is served on a pretty terrace in fine weather. 'Really helpful reception staff.' 'Good value.' Some rooms are small, some overlook the garden.

Open All year. **Rooms** 33 double, 3 single. **Facilities** Lifts. Breakfast room; terrace. **Location** *Centre historique*. Approach from W, via Promenade du Peyrou. Public car parks nearby (Peyrou-Piot, Foch). **Credit cards** All major cards accepted. **Terms** Room €71–€135. Breakfast €11.

LE JARDIN DES SENS   contemporary

11 avenue St-Lazare	*Tel* 00 33 4.99.58.38.38
Montpellier	*Fax* 00 33 4.99.58.38.39
34000 Hérault	*Email* contact@jardindessens.com
	Website www.jardindessens.com

'A very attractive, elegant hotel, pleasantly and efficiently staffed,' says a visitor to this ultra-modern restaurant-with rooms (three *Michelin* stars, 17 *Gault Millau* points; Relais & Châteaux). It may 'look like a fortress' from the front, but at the back, the huge three-level dining room has glass walls on three sides, facing an exotic Japanese-style garden. Brothers Jacques and Laurent Pourcel are owner/chefs, offering, eg, pigeon in pastilla with cocoa juice; pressé de homard aux jeunes légumes. 'The food was quite splendid,' one recent visitor wrote, though some have found the meal service 'a bit casual'. But breakfast was thought 'excellent'. The bedrooms, designed by an associate of Philippe Starck, have a Catalan influence (lots of red) and 'high-quality fixtures and fittings'.

Open All year, except Jan. Restaurant closed Sun/Mon midday, Wed midday, and Mon night/Tues midday except July/Aug. **Rooms** 2 suites, 12 double. **Facilities** Lift. Lounge, bar, restaurant. Garden: terrace, swimming pool. **Location** 1 km N of centre. Go towards Le Corum; take Nîmes road. Parking. **Credit cards** All major cards accepted. **Terms** Room €150–€250, suite €260–€450. Breakfast €15–€30. Set lunch €46, dinner €110–€170.

NANTES
(FlyBE)

The airport is just off the Nantes ring road.

HÔTEL DE LA BRETESCHE   luxury

Domaine de La Bretesche
Route de La Baule
Missillac
44780 Loire-Atlantique

Tel 00 33 2.51.76.86.96
Fax 00 33 2.40.66.99.47
Email hotel@bretesche.com
Website www.bretesche.com

Near La Baule, in a huge park with an 18-hole golf course and rhododendrons, stands this luxurious hotel (Relais & Châteaux), managed by Christophe Delahaye. It has been converted from the stable block of a moated medieval château, now uninhabited. 'Rooms are very comfortable,' says a recent visitor, 'particularly those with lake views. We thought the restaurant expensive, but the helpful reception staff introduced us to some super local eating places.' There is a flowery courtyard, a dining terrace, a swimming pool surrounded by hedges. *Gault Millau* awards 16 points for the eclectic cuisine of Gilles Charpy (eg, rabbit with mustard and cider; fillet of beef with polenta of mushrooms).

Open 1 Feb–12 Mar. Restaurant closed 7–23 Nov, Mon except 10 July–25 Aug, Tues midday, Sun night 15 Oct–15 Apr. **Rooms** 8 suites, 22 double. **Facilities** Lift. Lounge/bar, restaurant. **Location** 2 km NW of Missillac off N165 Nantes–Vannes. **Credit cards** All major cards accepted. **Terms** Room €130–€250, suite €250–€320. Breakfast €16. D,B&B €123–€307 per person.

CASTEL MARIE-LOUISE · belle époque

I avenue Andrieu
La Baule
44500 Loire-Atlantique

Tel 00 33 2.40.11.48.38
Fax 00 33 2.40.11.48.35
Email marielouise@relaischateaux.com
Website www.castel-marie-louise.com

'A marvellous hotel': the Barrière-Desseigne family's *belle époque* mansion stands in a large garden (with pine trees, white parasols and loungers) across the road from La Baule's magnificent beach. 'All the staff were superb (on our last day the concierge jump-started our flat car battery); we loved the relaxing atmosphere,' says a visitor. 'Our quiet, attractive room looked over the garden; its bathroom was well set out. We ate in the restaurant every night, the food was so good, as was the service' (*Michelin* star for Éric Mignard's classical cooking, eg, la poule 'coucou de Rennes' en gelée; blanc de merlu et langoustine croquante au basilic). There are antiques in public areas and in the bedrooms (some are large and sumptuous, with heavily patterned matching wallpaper and bedspread). Breakfast is 'a good buffet'. La Baule has water sports, riding, golf, a casino and a *Centre de Thalassothérapie*; the hotel offers an hour's free tennis each day for children, and bicycles are provided.

Open All year, except 14 Nov–18 Dec. Restaurant closed midday, except Sun, in low season. **Rooms** 2 suites, 29 double. **Facilities** Lift. Lobby, lounge, bar, restaurant. Terrace. Large garden. **Location** 1.5 km W of centre (shuttle available). Car park. **Credit cards** All major cards accepted. **Terms** Room €153–€455, suite €337–€525. Breakfast €18. D,B&B double €293–€665.

NICE

(bmibaby, easyJet, Jet2, Thomsonfly)

The airport is on the seafront,
6 km west of the city.

LE GRIMALDI	**Provençal comfort**

15 rue Grimaldi	*Tel* 00 33 4.93.16.00.24
06000 Nice	*Fax* 00 33 4.93.87.00.24
	Email zedde@le-grimaldi.com
	Website www.le-grimaldi.com

Down a quiet street near the old town and the seafront, Yann and Joanna Zedde (she is English) run a stylish and much-admired B&B in their *belle époque* house. They have doubled their capacity, up from 23 rooms to 46, by acquiring a nearby building, which forms a mirror image. Visitors found it 'very comfortable, quiet'. The *maison mère* has also won new praise: 'We loved it: friendly, high quality, with interesting decor.' Reception staff are 'friendly, unfailingly helpful'. The 'excellent' buffet breakfast includes freshly squeezed orange juice, fresh pastries; and you can boil your own eggs. All is neat and elegant: white-tiled bathrooms, bright colours, Provençal fabrics, flower and fruit prints on walls. All bathrooms have recently been renovated.

Open All year. **Rooms** 2 junior suites, 44 double. **Facilities** 2 lounge/bar/breakfast rooms; Internet centre. **Location** 4 blocks back from seafront, behind casino. **Credit cards** All major cards accepted. **Terms** Room: single €75–€155, double €85–€175, suite €190–€225. Breakfast €15.

LA PÉROUSE character

11 quai Rauba-Capeu
06300 Nice

Tel 00 33 4.93.62.34.63
Fax 00 33 4.93.62.59.41
Email lp@hroy.com
Website www.hroy.com/la-perouse

'The best all-round hotel experience I can remember' was enjoyed by a visitor to what is often called 'the best place to stay in Nice'. Superbly located, at the east end of the promenade, on a hillside below the castle, it has 'a world-class view across the Baie des Anges'. Newly refurbished in Provençal style, it also has character. 'A beautiful, very superior hotel, with charming staff, particularly the receptionists,' wrote inspectors. 'Our lovely room had tall windows leading on to a small balcony like a Matisse painting. A good marble bathroom. The big heated swimming pool is set below high rocks. On the charming terrace, with lemon trees, breakfast had good choice (quiche, fruit salad, etc).' On the roof is a solarium, with deckchairs and wide views; also a spa bath and small gym. The long corridors, painted yellow, are hung with marine and Impressionist prints. The building is set back from the busy road, so most rooms are quiet: some at the back have no view.

Open All year. Restaurant closed 20 Sept–10 May. **Rooms** 4 suites, 60 double, 2 single. **Facilities** Lifts. Lounge, bar, restaurant. Terrace: meal service. **Location** E end of Promenade des Anglais, by *Hôtel Suisse*. **Credit cards** All major cards accepted. **Terms** Room €150–€405, suite €580–€800. Breakfast €17.

HÔTEL WINDSOR   quirky

11 rue Dalpozzo   *Tel* 00 33 4.93.88.59.35
06000 Nice   *Fax* 00 33 4.93.88.94.57

Email reservation@hotelwindsornice.com
Website www.hotelwindsornice.com

'A delight,' say visitors to the Redolfi-Strizzot family's astonishing hotel, not far from the seafront, behind the mighty *Hôtel Negresco*. Convenient, fairly quiet, yet lively, it is full of 'the quirky furnishings of an eclectic collector'. 'I loved the lift that says "seven, six, five, start main engines, four, three, two, one, lift off". Then the doors open.' The 'splendid Moroccan garden', 'overgrown, charming', has taped ('rather scratchy') birdsong and a very small swimming pool. Many bedrooms have been painted by artists: 'Mine had an amazing naïve painting of an Indian scene, in lovely pastel colours.' 'Ours was spacious, with good beds, but the bathroom door did not close, and the smart Italian bathroom fittings were not entirely functional.' 'A delightful hotel. Charming young staff. A minimalist white room, very comfortable. We enjoyed dinner in the panelled dining room, where a fire was lit. Breakfast was good.' 'In late October, dinner outdoors, with pretty lights in the trees, was delightful. Good food and charming service.' The small bar is 'congenial'.

Open All year. Restaurant closed Sun. **Rooms** 57 double. **Facilities** Lounge/bar, restaurant; fitness centre, hammam, sauna. Garden: dining terrace. **Location** Central, 400 m from Promenade des Anglais. **Credit cards** All major cards accepted. **Terms** Room €75–€155. Breakfast €8. D,B&B: single €103–€183, double €131–€211.

NÎMES
(Ryanair)

The airport is 12 km south-east of the town.

LA PASSIFLORE   value

1 rue Neuve   *Tel* 00 33 4.66.35.00.00
Vergèze   *Fax* 00 33 4.66.35.09.21
30310 Gard

Run by its 'exceptionally nice' owners, Anthony and Linda
Booth, this Logis de France is a creeper-covered old
farmhouse, in a village south of Nîmes, near the A9. All the
bedrooms face a courtyard or garden: some are small, and
their lighting may be poor. One couple found the exterior
'unprepossessing' and the reception 'confusing', but fans
(many visitors are English) love the 'sheer cosiness' and good
value. The 'above-average' dinner, cooked by Mrs Booth, is
served by candlelight, in the 'delightful small dining room'
with its large fireplace, or in the courtyard in summer. The
host is 'entertaining, helpful, very professional'. Surprisingly,
breakfast is 'typical French nothing', sometimes served in a
'characterless foyer'.

Open All year. Restaurant closed midday, 1 Oct–31 Mar, Sun,
Mon. **Rooms** 11 double. **Facilities** Lounge, breakfast room,
restaurant. Courtyard, garden. **Location** Village 20 km SW of
Nîmes. Parking. **Credit cards** Amex, MasterCard, Visa. **Terms**
Room €42–€60. Breakfast €7. D,B&B (min. 3 days): single €68–€84,
double €98–€114.

LE VIEUX CASTILLON   luxury

Rue Turion Sabatier
Castillon-du-Gard
30210 Gard

Tel 00 33 4.66.37.61.61
Fax 00 33 4.66.37.28.17
Email vieux.castillon@wanadoo.fr
Website www.relaischateaux.com

'Our favourite hotel, so comfortable, with such helpful staff,' says a visitor to the Walser family's ever-admired, luxurious Relais & Châteaux member. It is a conversion, 'with charm and imagination', of a group of ancient houses in a 'delightful' hill village near the Pont du Gard. The flowery garden, where breakfasts can be taken, is sheltered from the mistral; the terrace and the large, beautiful swimming pool enjoy wide views over a plain with vineyards. Across a bridge is the beamed restaurant, where Gilles Dauteuil's 'contemporary Mediterranean cooking' wins a *Michelin* star. 'The dinners were very, very good, but in an elaborate way that might pall; there are, however, several cheaper restaurants nearby. Breakfasts of high quality, but the speed of their service varied.' 'Though two clocks can be heard, this is a peaceful place.' Bedrooms vary in size and quality: most are elegant, with period furniture and flowery fabrics; some look over a narrow village street. In the lounge are wooden floors, oriental rugs and striped armchairs.

Open Mid-Feb–end Dec. Restaurant closed midday on Mon and Tues. **Rooms** 2 junior suites, 31 double. **Facilities** 2 salons, TV room, bar, restaurant; billiards, sauna, hammam. **Location** 4 km N of the Pont du Gard, 26 km W of Avignon. Parking 300 m (€15 a night). **Credit cards** All major cards accepted. **Terms** Room €175–€289, suite €315. Breakfast €16. D,B&B €105 added per person.

PARIS
(bmibaby, easyJet, FlyBE, Ryanair)

Bmibaby, easyJet and FlyBE fly to Charles de Gaulle
at Roissy, 23 km north-east. Ryanair flies to
Beauvais, which is 56 km north-west.

HÔTEL D'ANGLETERRE   traditional

44 rue Jacob   *Tel* 00 33 1.42.60.34.72
75006 Paris   *Fax* 00 33 1.42.60.16.93
                              Email anglotel@wanadoo.fr

A handsome old house, near St-Germain des Prés, once the
British Embassy and now a hotel of character. 'Helpful
reception staff, attractive salon [with piano, and newspapers
on wooden sticks] and breakfast room. Our interconnecting
bedrooms, wonderfully large and characterful, had beamed
high ceilings, comfy sofas and beds, old fireplaces; large
bathrooms with attractive old-style fittings.' 'Our room, very
quiet, faced the attractive courtyard with tables and chairs.'
'Very good buffet breakfast, included in the room price.'
Earlier praise: 'The old entrance door, the tiled foyer are
delightful. This compensates for the dusty gentility of
corridors, and staircases steep and rickety. The bedrooms
are of varied styles and sizes: furnished traditionally, antiques
scattered about.'

Open All year. **Rooms** 4 suites, 22 double, 1 single. **Facilities**
Lift. Lounge, breakfast room. **Location** Central. (Métro: Hotel de
Ville) **Credit cards** All major cards accepted. **Terms** B&B: single
€135–€230, double €145–€240, suite €280–€320.

CHÂTILLON HÔTEL   budget

11 square de Châtillon	*Tel* 00 33 1.45.42.31.17
75014 Paris	*Fax* 00 33 1.45.42.72.09
	Email chatillon.hotel@wanadoo.fr

Offering 'perhaps the best value in Paris', Luce and Bernard Lecoq's very personal little hotel has an offbeat location, in an 'amazingly quiet' square down near the Porte d'Orléans. But transport links to the centre are good. Cheerful and pleasantly quirky, simple and without frills, it is 'frequented by cultured French people' and 'does not have a touristy feel'. 'Madame is charming, very hands-on'; her husband 'makes superb coffee'. 'The rooms were most comfortable,' says a visitor. They are roomy, with furniture 'in Habitat 1970s style'; all have big windows and a spacious white bathroom. 'A filling breakfast, with a newspaper.' 'Very peaceful', 'you can hear the birds sing' – but also the early dustbin vans. Recommended local restaurants (both *Michelin Bib Gourmand*): *La Régalade*, avenue Jean Moulin; *La Bonne Table*, rue Friant.

Open All year. **Rooms** 31 double. 1 on ground floor. **Facilities** Lift. Lounge, bar/TV room, breakfast room. **Location** Entrance to square by 33 ave Jean Moulin. Garage parking nearby. (Métro: Alésia) **Credit cards** MasterCard, Visa. **Terms** Room: single/double €62. Breakfast €6.

HÔTEL CHOPIN   value

10 boulevard Montmartre	*Tel* 00 33 1.47.70.58.10
(46 passage Jouffroy)	*Fax* 00 33 1.42.47.00.70
75009 Paris	

'It is staggeringly good value for central Paris,' says a returning visitor to Philippe Bidal's modest hotel. Set at the end of a picturesque, glass-roofed, 19th-century arcade with shops, off the Grands Boulevards, it proudly notes that it has been open for business every day of the year since 1846. Many bedrooms and bathrooms are small, but as one reader pointed out: 'We don't all want the pricier luxury places.' Another visitor was 'almost reluctant to say how good the *Chopin* is'. Among its charms are the 'cheerful staff', 'faded elegance'. 'The quietest hotel we have found in Paris.' There are some idiosyncrasies such as creaky lifts and antiquated plumbing. The buffet breakfast is generally liked: it has an electric juice maker and 'plentiful, good hot coffee'. *Chartier*, 7 rue du Faubourg Montmartre, one of Paris's best traditional budget restaurants, is nearby: 'Not tranquil, it buzzes with life and like as not you will have to share your table.'

Open All year. **Rooms** 31 double, 5 single. **Facilities** Lift. Reception, breakfast room. **Location** Central. Public parking Rue Chauchat. (Métro: Richelieu-Drouot) **Credit cards** Amex, MasterCard, Visa. **Terms** Room €63–€97. Breakfast €7.

RELAIS CHRISTINE   luxury

3 rue Christine
75006 Paris

Tel 00 33 1.40.51.60.80
Fax 00 33 1.40.51.60.81
Email contact@relais-christine.com
Website www.relais-christine.com

Down a side street near the Seine, this luxurious hotel, 'lovely in every respect', is a converted 16th-century mansion on the site of an Augustinian abbey. Recent comments: 'Service is impeccable.' 'A wonderful atmosphere.' 'Like a small country house. Our room looked over the garden, where the only noise was the birds' dawn chorus.' Some bedrooms have a terrace by the 'charming garden'; some others face the courtyard, with its topiary shrubs and magnolia. Some front rooms might get a night chorus of cinema-goers. Some rooms are small, but all are well furnished, with 'sumptuous' fabrics; many have beams. A buffet breakfast is served in the vaulted former refectory; even the continental breakfast is 'generous and delicious'. The panelled lounge has an honesty bar, board games, English newspapers and a log fire; guests have the use of a computer with Internet access.

Open All year. **Rooms** 16 suites, 35 double. **Facilities** Lounge with honesty bar, breakfast room; spa (fitness room, sauna, massage, etc). Small garden. **Location** Left Bank. (Métro: Odéon, St-Michel) **Credit cards** All major cards accepted. **Terms** Room €335–€430. Breakfast €20–€25.

HÔTEL MONTALEMBERT   ultra-modern

3 rue de Montalembert   *Tel* 00 33 1.45.49.68.68
75007 Paris   *Fax* 00 33 1.45.49.69.49
                          Email welcome@montalembert.com
                          Website www.montalembert.com

Ultra-modern, with cutting edge technology, the *Montalembert*, near Boulevard St-Germain, is managed by Alexandre Fougerole. The latest make-over by Grace Leo-Andrieu has made it 'super-trendy, a fascinating mix of modern and traditional styles', reports an admirer. It has gleaming marble floors, dramatic flower displays, a colour scheme of taupe, olive and cinnamon, and a 'very Art Deco' design in its public areas. Staff wear a 'Prada-style sand-and-gunpowder-grey uniform'. 'Service is very friendly.' Every bedroom has a flat-screen TV, DVD-player and Internet access; 'well appointed, if small', they have Louis Philippe or 'resolutely contemporary' decor and a marble and chrome bathroom. The top-floor suites have spectacular views. The bar/grill serves breakfast and, unusually for Paris, light meals all day. In the oak-panelled restaurant, the chef, Alain Lecompte, allows guests to 'compose their own menu and decide size of portion'. The outdoor dining terrace has 'Alice in Wonderland-style banquettes', camellias and box trees.

Open All year. **Rooms** 8 suites, 48 double. **Facilities** Salon, bar/café, restaurant, terrace. **Location** Near junction of blvds St-Germain/Raspail/rue du Bac. (Métro: Rue du Bac) **Credit cards** All major cards accepted. **Terms** Room €320–€450, suite €490–€1,150. Breakfast €20.

HÔTEL DE VIGNY   chic

9–11 rue Balzac
75008 Paris

Tel 00 33 1.42.99.80.80
Fax 00 33 1.42.99.80.40
Email reservation@hoteldevigny.com
Website www.hoteldevigny.com

'An excellent base in Paris', this Relais & Châteaux hotel is in a quiet side street between the Champs-Élysées and avenue de Friedland. Small and luxurious, it has a Nina Campbell decor and 'comfy English chic'. Regular visitors return because 'it gave us a feeling of being at home'. 'Uncharacteristically for an expensive hotel, the staff were charming,' writes a recent visitor. A log fire burns in the wood-panelled lobby where guests are informally welcomed at a desk; off it is a small salon. Bedrooms are 'excellent', though one reader 'had to climb into the bath to reach the taps'; another had a whirlpool bath. Film stars often visit. The associated *Baretto* restaurant, Art Deco in style, with leather armchairs, serves 'excellent breakfasts and good, modest meals'.

Open All year, except perhaps 15 days in Aug. **Rooms** 11 suites, 25 double, 1 single. **Facilities** Large lobby, library, bar, restaurant. **Location** Near Étoile (windows double-glazed). (Métro: George V) **Credit cards** All major cards accepted. **Terms** Room from €395, junior suite from €620, suite from €725. Breakfast €21–€28.

PAU
(Ryanair)

The airport is 7 km north of Pau.

HÔTEL CHILO   smart dining

Barcus   *Tel* 00 33 5.59.28.90.79
64130 Pyrénées-Atlantiques   *Fax* 00 33 5.59.28.93.10
                              Email martine.chilo@wanadoo.fr
                              Website www.hotel-chilo.com

In a village not far from Pau, on the eastern edge of the Pays Basque, this old inn has been turned by owner/chef Pierre Chilo into a smart restaurant-with-rooms. 'Remarkable value, excellent food,' runs recent praise (but one visitor found the welcome cool). *Gault Millau* gives 14 points for the regional cuisine, served lavishly. You can dine by the fireside in winter, on a terrace by the flowery garden in summer. 'Gentle, attractive furnishings.' 'A good-sized bedroom with a marvellous view.' Bedrooms and bathrooms vary in size; some were recently redecorated. But upkeep can be imperfect, while cheaper annexe rooms are said to be 'basic'.

Open All year, except 3 weeks Jan, 1 week Feb. Restaurant closed Sun evening/Mon, Tues midday in low season. **Rooms** 1 suite, 10 double. **Facilities** 2 salons, bar, restaurant. Garden: swimming pool. **Location** Village centre, 18 km W of Oloron-Ste-Marie. **Credit cards** All major cards accepted. **Terms** Room: single €32–€74, double €43–€85, suite €79–€100. Breakfast €8. D,B&B €59–€103 per person.

PERPIGNAN
(FlyBE, Ryanair)

The airport is 5 km north-east of the
French Catalan capital.

HÔTEL MADELOC   **budget**

24 rue Romain-Rolland	*Tel* 00 33 4.68.82.07.56
Collioure	*Fax* 00 33 4.68.82.55.09
66190 Pyrénées-Orientales	*Email* hotel@madeloc.com
	Website www.madeloc.com

Matisse, Dufy and others often visited and painted this colourful old fishing port near the Spanish border. Away from the crowded waterfront, the Pouchairet-Ramona family's B&B hotel, 'not luxurious, but good value', is up a steep side street. 'You feel part of the family,' says a devotee. 'Christine, her husband and mother-in-law all seem genuinely interested in your well-being; son Jean-Laurent and two dogs complete the picture. My third-floor room, up steep stairs, had French windows opening on to its own little terrace, surrounded by lavender bushes. The views over the mountains are beautiful, especially as the sun sets.' Public areas have Catalan paintings. There is a large high-ceilinged reception area, and a 'pleasant, smallish' swimming pool with a service bar.

Open 15 Mar–1 Nov. **Rooms** 22 double. Some with terrace. **Facilities** Bar/breakfast room. Garden. **Location** 500 m from centre. 29 km SE of Perpignan. Garage. Parking. **Credit cards** All major cards accepted. **Terms** Room €58–€89. Breakfast €7.

LA TERRASSE AU SOLEIL   Catalan

Route de Fontfrède	*Tel* 00 33 4.68.87.01.94
Céret	*Fax* 00 33 4.68.87.39.24
66400 Pyrénées-Orientales	*Email* terrasse-au-soleil.hotel@
	wanadoo.fr
	Website www.la-terrasse-au-soleil.fr

This little town in the Pyrenean foothills south of Perpignan is renowned for its cherries, and this old *mas*, just outside, stands amid cherry orchards: its restaurant is called *La Cerisaie*. Run by the Leveillé-Nizerolle family, it was enjoyed again by most recent visitors: 'The setting and view are glorious, and there is a delightful small garden. We liked the heated pool, the copious breakfasts and the excellently prepared and presented food. More of a restaurant-with-rooms than a hotel (our annexe rooms were motel-like).' Another couple had 'a large, comfortable room, and a balcony with an amazing view'. But one visitor found management 'unhelpful'. The decor is in vivid Catalan style, and some dishes are Catalan. In summer, guests are expected to dine in. One guest thought the food 'over-elaborate', and extras can be expensive. The staff are thought 'charming'. Best to arrive in daylight: 'The approach road is tortuous and narrow.' Céret's museum contains works by Matisse, Chagall, Picasso, etc, all of whom lived and painted in the area.

Open All year. Restaurant closed midday, except Sat and Sun. **Rooms** 7 suites, 31 double. Some in 4 annexes. **Facilities** 2 lounges, bar, restaurant; breakfast room. **Location** 1.5 km W of Céret, 31 km SW of Perpignan. Parking. **Credit cards** All major cards accepted. **Terms** B&B: single €110–€217, double €159–€265, suite €190–€296; D,B&B €110–€247 per person.

POITIERS
(Ryanair)

The airport is just outside the town.

RELAIS DU LYON D'OR   budget

4 rue d'Enfer
Angles-sur-l'Anglin
86260 Vienne

Tel 00 33 5.49.48.32.53
Fax 00 33 5.49.84.02.28
Email thoreau@lyondor.com
Website www.lyondor.com

In this 'stunning' village east of Poitiers, an Anglo-French couple, Heather and Guillaume Thoreau, have restored this creeper-covered 15th-century inn from a derelict state. It is 'a treasure', run with style, says one visitor. Others wrote of the 'welcoming atmosphere'. 'Our beamed bedroom had stencilled walls, some antique furniture, a lovely patchwork bedspread. In the attractive beamed dining room, a log fire burned; the tablecloths matched the terracotta floor tiles.' 'A superb dinner.' 'Residents get a fine buffet dinner, cooked by Heather, on Mondays. Breakfast was pleasant': others called it 'excellent'. Served on the terrace on fine days, it includes home-baked croissants, and (for a supplement) eggs. Bedrooms, round a courtyard, are decorated to reflect aspects of the village.

Open Mar–Dec. Restaurant closed to non-residents Mon/Tues midday. **Rooms** 2 suites, 9 double. **Facilities** Salon/reception, games/TV room, restaurant; 2 terraces. Garden. **Location** Village centre. 34 km SE of Châtellerault. Parking. **Credit cards** Amex, MasterCard, Visa. **Terms** Room: double €55–€80, suite €90–€100. Breakfast €8. D,B&B (min. 3 nights) €60–€83 per person.

DOMAINE DE L'ÉTAPE   rural

Route de Bélâbre
Le Blanc
36300 Indre

Tel 00 33 2.54.37.18.02
Fax 00 33 2.54.37.75.59
Email domainetape@wanadoo.fr
Website www.domaineetape.com

'As fine as ever': a returning visitor again loved Nicole Seiller's 19th-century *belle demeure bourgeoise*. It stands up a long drive in a huge park, with horses and a lake for fishing and boating, down a country lane east of Poitiers. The 'quiet location', 'old-fashioned' aura, and welcome to children are all enjoyed. The bedrooms vary: some, 'up a lot of stairs', are on the maids' floor, 'still with service bells in the corridors'. One visitor had 'a lovely big attic room'. Other rooms ('quite basic') are in modern *pavillons* and (the cheapest: 'not fancy, but comfortable') in a farmhouse. 'The gourmet menu was delicious and copious. There are cheaper menus, too, and a *petite carte* with favourites like potage maison, served by the gallon in tureens.' 'Wonderful desserts, sumptuous cheeseboard.' The continental breakfast is 'more than pleasant'. '*La patronne* is magnificent'; her manager is Pascal Faure. There is a terrace for summer meals. Lots of wildlife nearby, in the Parc de la Brenne.

Open All year. **Rooms** 35 double. **Facilities** Lounge with TV, 2 dining rooms. 220-hectare park. **Location** 5 km SE of Le Blanc, off D10 to Bélâbre, 60 km E of Poitiers. **Credit cards** All major cards accepted. **Terms** Room €38–€105. Breakfast €9. Set meals €20–€54; full alc €45.

LA ROCHELLE
(FlyBE, Ryanair)

The airport is close to the Île de Ré,
the popular holiday island.

HÔTEL RESTAURANT L'OCÉAN   seaside

---

172 rue de St-Martin   *Tel* 00 33 5.46.09.23.07
Le Bois-Plage-en-Ré   *Fax* 00 33 5.46.09.05.40
Île de Ré   *Email* info@re-hotel-ocean.com
17580 Charente-Maritime   *Website* www.re-hotel-ocean.com

Offshore from enchanting La Rochelle, the long Île de Ré, with its white beaches, is a favourite French holiday venue. Here, Noël and Martine Bourdet's popular two-star Logis de France is 'busy even in April' (advance booking essential). It has 'a seaside ambience and a rural charm': it is 500 metres from the beach, in a 'pretty, sleepy village'. 'I loved it,' said a recent visitor. A swimming pool is being built, and there are four large new bedrooms; some other rooms look over the garden; some are very small. The public rooms are 'attractive in a hip-seaside way'. Meals are served in the beamed restaurant or on a patio: the chef, Yoann Leraut, specialises in fish. Breakfast is a buffet.

Open All year, except 24/25 Dec, 4 Jan–9 Feb, Wed except school holidays. **Rooms** 28 double, 2 single. **Facilities** Salon, bar, restaurant. **Location** In village, halfway along island. 23 km W of La Rochelle. **Credit cards** Amex, MasterCard, Visa. **Terms** Room €61–€91. Breakfast €10. D,B&B €61.50–€108 per person.

LE CORPS DE GARDE   stylish

I quai Georges Clemenceau   *Tel* 00 33 5.46.09.10.50
St-Martin-de-Ré   *Fax* 00 33 5.46.09.76.99
Île de Ré   *Email* info@lecorpsdegarde.com
17410 Charente-Maritime   *Website* www.lecorpsdegarde.com

'The setting could not be more picturesque': on this holiday island, this former coastguard's house, with its wide ocean views, is now a 'supremely stylish' *maison d'hôtes*. 'Memorable, very comfortable', it stands on the corner of the quay, sea and fortifications on one side, harbour full of boats on the other. The decor is '*fait dans un esprit de maison de famille*', say the owners, M. and Mme Bressy. Each room is different, decorated with light colours, natural fabrics, seagrass matting and plain wood. All have a view; most have a sitting area and sofa. Good insulation. The salon, in the former boathouse, has an open fire, potted plants. Breakfast is served here, or in the bedroom, '*sans limite d'heure*'. Plenty of restaurants at the port.

Open All year. **Rooms** 5 double. **Facilities** Salon. **Location** By harbour. **Credit cards** MasterCard, Visa. **Terms** Room €90–€180. Breakfast €10. 1-night bookings refused holiday weekends.

LE RICHELIEU   luxury

44 avenue de la Plage	*Tel* 00 33 5.46.09.60.70
La Flotte	*Fax* 00 33 5.46.09.50.59
Île de Ré	*Email* info@hotel-le-richelieu.com
17630 Charente-Maritime	*Website* www.hotel-le-richelieu.com

'We love it,' say visitors to the Gendre family's sybaritic modern white paradise (Relais & Châteaux) on the Atlantic coast of the holiday island of Ré. It stands across the road from a beach: tides go far out, and bathing can be shallow. The bedrooms have period furnishings; many have a wide terrace facing the sea; some are in bungalows in the 'very private' garden. 'Our middle-price room, beautifully decorated, had murals of ships and rural scenes painted on whitewashed panelled walls. The public areas are well done, luxurious yet relaxing. There is a small library. Splendid stained glass includes a depiction of Richelieu above the lovely staircase. Staff were helpful; dinner was very good, with an emphasis on shellfish and fresh seafood. Puddings were perfect. The half-board guests were herded into one part of the dining room, but service was attentive.' *Michelin* awards a star for dishes like langoustines grillées à la laque d'épices. The gardens are lovely, too; the swimming pool is large, with loungers.

Open All year, except Jan. **Rooms** 6 suites, 34 double. 24 in 2 annexes. **Facilities** Lounge, bar, restaurant; thalassotherapy centre. **Location** NE coast of island (16 km NW of airport). **Credit cards** Amex, MasterCard, Visa. **Terms** D,B&B €125–€305.

RODEZ
(Ryanair)

The airport is close to the town, a gateway
to the attractive Aveyron hill villages.

HÔTEL SAINTE-FOY   cosy inn

Rue Principale   *Tel* 00 33 5.65.69.84.03
Conques   *Fax* 00 33 5.65.72.81.04
12320 Aveyron   *Email* hotelsaintefoy@hotelsaintefoy.fr
                            Website www.hotelsaintefoy.fr

This 'lovely place' is the Garcenot family's 17th-century
timbered inn in this 'magical village', on a wooded hillside
above a gorge, some 30 km from the airport at Rodez. It
stands opposite the famous and splendid abbey. 'Old stones
and rustic furniture' add to its 'cosy feel'. 'Most of the staff
are female.' One couple had a 'big, handsome' front room
facing the abbey. Others wrote of 'a delicious dinner,
beautifully presented, eagerly explained by the young wife of
the chef, Laurent Dufour', with dishes like escalopes de foie
gras de canard poêlées. There is a pretty garden dining area,
and a more formal beamed dining room.

Open Easter–1 Nov. **Rooms** 2 suites, 15 double. **Facilities** Lift,
ramp. Lounges, TV lounge, bar, 3 dining rooms; patio; rooftop
terrace. **Location** Central, opposite abbey church. 5 garages.
Credit cards All major cards accepted. **Terms** Room
€100–€189, suite €199–€210. Breakfast €14. D,B&B: single
€191–€235, double €205–€280.

HÔTEL RESTAURANT DU VIEUX PONT   gourmet

Belcastel
12390 Aveyron

Tel 00 33 5.65.64.52.29
Fax 00 33 5.65.64.44.32
Email hotel-du-vieux-pont@wanadoo.fr
Website www.hotelbelcastel.com

'Staggering food with the greatest pride and concern for excellence.' 'It has a happy air.' Much praise for an inspired rural success story – the ever-admired restaurant which the Fagegaltier sisters converted from their family home in the 1980s. It stands amid 'rich countryside' in an old Massif Central hamlet, designated 'one of France's most beautiful villages', which rises on the sides of a steep cliff topped by a feudal castle. The *Vieux Pont* sits beside a 15th-century cobbled bridge over the swift-flowing Aveyron. It used to be the village café. Today, Michèle is the elegant front-of-house, while Nicole and her husband, Bruno Rouquier, win a *Michelin* star, 15 *Gault Millau* points for their regional cooking. The food is 'fantastically presented', 'sophisticated, yet refreshingly simple', in a room with 'a relaxed upmarket chic' and picture windows facing the river. The tiny hotel is across the bridge, with a 'delightful' little garden, and 'imaginatively designed', spacious, modern bedrooms (white walls, curtains and bedspreads, wooden floors). 'Excellent breakfasts by the river.'

Open 15 Mar–31 Dec. Closed 25 Dec midday. **Rooms** 7 double. **Facilities** Restaurant; terrace. Garden. **Location** Centre of village. 23 km W of Rodez, off D994 to Villefranche. **Credit cards** MasterCard, Visa. **Terms** Room €72–€85. Breakfast €12. D,B&B €88–€124 per person.

CHÂTEAU DU VIGUIER DU ROY   historic

52 rue Droite   *Tel* 00 33 5.65.50.05.05
Figeac   *Fax* 00 33 5.65.50.06.06
46100 Lot   *Email* hotel@chateau-viguier-figeac.com
Website www.chateau-viguier-figeac.com

'We thoroughly enjoyed our stay in this lovely old hotel,' visitors write. In the ancient heart of a beautiful town in the Quercy, amid a maze of alleys, it is a fascinating ensemble of buildings from the 12th, 14th and 18th centuries – 'a delight to explore'. Once the home of a local governor, it has a colonnaded exterior, a medieval keep, a vaulted Gothic chapel, and a tiny swimming pool behind the lovely cloister. All has been 'intelligently restored' by the owner/manager, Anne Secordel-Martin. 'A splendid dinner': chef Daniel Authié provides *cuisine du terroir*, 'served flamboyantly, but without pretension', in a beamed room with a huge carved stone fireplace, or in the tiny courtyard. Bedrooms vary in size; some are huge, with period furniture. 'Our interconnecting rooms, facing the main street, were a delight.' 'Ours, high up, was light, with a long balcony, views to the cathedral, and hills across the river. Luxurious white four-poster bed.' Bathrooms are modern. Breakfast, in a vaulted room, offers plenty of choice.

Open 9 Apr–24 Oct. **Rooms** 2 apartments, 3 suites, 16 double. **Facilities** Lift. Lounges, library, bar, 3 dining rooms. **Location** Central. Figeac is 63 km NW of Rodez. **Credit cards** All major cards accepted. **Terms** Room €130–€200, suite €245–€375. Breakfast €14–€17. Set meals €25–€60; full alc €36–€69.

ST-ÉTIENNE
(Ryanair)

The airport is close to the town. Ryanair
promotes it as an entry point to Lyon, 75 km away.
Our selections are in the southern Rhône valley.

HÔTEL RESTAURANT LE BELLEVUE   *riverside*

Quai du Rhône	*Tel* 00 33 4.74.56.41.42
Les Roches-de-Condrieu	*Fax* 00 33 4.74.56.47.56
38370 Isère	*Website* www.federal-hotel.com

A 'small, welcoming' hotel, modern and creeper-covered,
right beside the majestically curving Rhône, in a village south
of Lyon. 'The new owners, Josiane and Jean Paret, have
freshened things up,' says a returning visitor. 'Their staff
were friendly. As so often in France, the emphasis was on
the food. In the pleasant restaurant, with its huge fireplace
and large windows facing the river, we ate very well.
Coquilles St-Jacques and beef were particularly enjoyed.
Substantial buffet breakfast.' On an earlier visit she liked her
large room: 'From its balcony, with seating, we enjoyed
looking at the river and the vineyards beyond.'

Open All year. **Rooms** 3 suites, 13 double. **Facilities** Salon, bar,
restaurant. **Location** 13 km SW of Vienne. On river, by marina.
Safe parking. **Credit cards** MasterCard, Visa. **Terms** Room
€50–€70. Breakfast €8. Set meals €26–€49.

DOMAINE DE CLAIREFONTAINE   country

Chemin des Fontanettes   *Tel* 00 33 4.74.58.81.52
Chonas l'Amballan   *Fax* 00 33 4.74.58.80.93
38121 Isère   *Email* domaine.de.clairefontaine@gofornet.com
                             Website domaine-de-clairefontaine.fr

'Wonderfully relaxing', 'the food was fantastic, my room large and comfortable' – more praise for this country hotel: a 'lovely 18th-century mansion' (though one dissenter found the restaurant manager unfriendly and reception staff 'unhelpful'). Once the country home of the bishops of Lyon, on the edge of a Rhône valley village, it has a big garden with a pond and birdsong, and is owned and run by the Girardon family. The terrace facing the gardens is 'beautiful'; the restaurant is stylishly decorated in yellow, with grey marble floors. Chef Philippe Girardon's *Michelin*-starred dishes include soupière de grenouilles et mousserons à l'ail des ours. 'The *amuse-bouche* exploded with taste in my mouth', 'the chocolate desserts have to be seen to be believed'. The renovated annexe, *Les Jardins de Clairefontaine*, is 'sophisticated, with a sleek lift, automatic sliding glass doors, electronically operated shutters, smart bathrooms'. Bedrooms in the main house are now being upgraded.

Open All year, except 15 Dec–15 Jan, 1 May. **Rooms** 2 suites, 26 double. **Facilities** Lift. Salon/bar, 2 dining rooms. **Location** 9 km SW of Vienne: from N, leave *autoroute* at Condrieu, then follow N7; from S, leave *autoroute* at exit 12, then follow N7. **Credit cards** All major cards accepted. **Terms** Room €48–€105. Breakfast €13. Set meals €42–€120; full alc €70.

STRASBOURG
(FlyBE)

The airport is 15 km south-west of the city.

HÔTEL CARDINAL DE ROHAN   central

17–19 rue du Maroquin   *Tel* 00 33 3.88.32.85.11
Strasbourg   *Fax* 00 33 3.88.75.65.37
67000 Bas-Rhin   *Email* info@hotel-rohan.com
                               Website www.hotel-rohan.com

In the traffic-free zone by the cathedral, Rolf van Maenen's spruce B&B hotel is 'wonderfully located'. The welcome is by 'smiling, helpful' receptionists and porters. 'Cosy lounges' have tapestries and chandeliers. Many bedrooms are quite small; some are in Louis XV or rustic style. They are air-conditioned and double-glazed, but street noise and the cathedral bells can be heard until late. 'Good breakfasts' (fresh fruit, etc). Many restaurants nearby: *L'Ami Fritz*, in the pretty Petite France, is much liked.

Open All year. **Rooms** 28 double, 8 single. **Facilities** Lift. Reception, salons, 2 breakfast rooms. **Location** Pedestrian zone by cathedral. **Credit cards** All major cards accepted. **Terms** Room: single €63–€107, double €92–€122. Breakfast €10.

HÔTEL DU DRAGON   minimalist

2 rue de l'Écarlate	*Tel* 00 33 3.88.35.79.80
Strasbourg	*Fax* 00 33 3.88.25.78.95
67000 Bas-Rhin	*Email* hotel@dragon.fr
	Website www.dragon.fr

'I still love the *Dragon*,' says a fan returning to this B&B hotel in the charming old centre of this busy city. A 17th-century house in a quiet cul-de-sac, it has a modern 'minimalist' decor. 'My room was soothing in pale grey and cream. Small attic windows looked over cathedral on one side, top floors of houses on the other, giving a pleasant feel of being part of the community.' Another visitor wrote of the hotel's 'good atmosphere'. The 'very cordial' owner, Jean Zimmer, runs it with a 'charming team'. On the front courtyard (with plants in terracotta pots), breakfast (with fresh fruit and yogurt, boiled egg), drinks and light lunches are served. Recommended restaurants include *Maison des Tanneurs* and *Zum Strissel*.

Open All year. **Rooms** 2 suites, 30 double. **Facilities** Lift. Salon, bar, breakfast room. Courtyard. **Location** Central: off Quai St-Nicolas, near Pl. d'Austerlitz. Public car park; 4 private spaces. **Credit cards** All major cards accepted. **Terms** Room €69–€112, suite (3 or 4 people) €129–€145. Breakfast €9.50.

TOULOUSE
(bmibaby, easyJet, FlyBE)

The airport is 8 km north-west of the city.

CHÂTEAU CAP DE CASTEL château

Le Bourg	*Tel/Fax* 00 33 5.63.70.21.76
Puylaurens	*Email* hotel@chateau-capdecastel.com
81700 Tarn	*Website* www.chateau-capdecastel.com

'Delightful: family-run, welcoming, tastefully decorated and clean', this converted 13th-century château, with bedrooms in two 17th-century buildings, is in the old centre of this former *albigeois* stronghold, 58 km east of Toulouse. It has 'fabulous views' over surrounding countryside. 'We were shown,' says a visitor, 'to enormous high-ceilinged rooms, with antiques. Bathrooms are spacious. Simple furnishings, but no tat.' Meals are served on the 'lovely terrace' by the small swimming pool, or in a room with a large fireplace. Ingredients include 'meat from pigs raised *en plein air* and deer in *semi-liberté*'. 'Evening meal a bit overpriced, but good and cheery service and the wonderful location made up for this. Basic breakfast, but bread was fresh and croissants were hot.'

Open All year, except Nov. **Rooms** 11 bedrooms (including family suite). **Facilities** Salon, restaurant. Garden: dining terrace. **Location** Centre of town. Public garage nearby. **Credit cards** Diners, MasterCard, Visa. **Terms** Room €39–€82, suite €99. Breakfast €6. Set meals €14–€20.

HÔTEL DES CAPITOULS   modern

22 descente de la Halle aux Poissons
Toulouse   *Tel* 00 33 5.34.31.94.80
31000 Haute-Garonne   *Fax* 00 33 5.34.31.94.81
                            Email contact@hoteldescapitouls.com
                            Website www.hoteldescapitouls.com

'Distinctive and impressive', this newly opened small hotel, in a small, quiet side street in the medieval city, is 'unreservedly recommended': 'Very special; extremely well appointed.' The decor is modern, with lots of red, contemporary artwork. Drinks are served in the lounge. Two bedrooms have views of the Garonne. A continental breakfast is brought to the bedrooms, and a buffet breakfast can be taken in the 'fine' restaurant opposite, *Le 19*, under the same ownership. In a vaulted cellar, 'it has two dining rooms, a remarkably comprehensive Toulouse wine cellar and, shades of Old England, a smokers' lounge'. The owner, Pierre Courtois de Viçose, also owns the cheaper *Hôtel des Beaux Arts* nearby (19 bedrooms). Also nearby is the Hôtel d'Assézat, a glorious Renaissance mansion, now a cultural centre.

Open All year. Restaurant closed Sat midday, Sun/Mon midday, Christmas/New Year. **Rooms** 3 suites, 11 double, 1 single. **Facilities** Lobby, lounge, restaurant (30 m). **Location** Central, near river (windows double-glazed). Public underground car park (200 m). **Credit cards** Amex, MasterCard, Visa. **Terms** Room €134–€173, suite €205–€267. Breakfast €16. Set lunch €17–€20, dinner €29–€39.

TOURS
(Ryanair)

The airport is 6 km north of the city.

CHÂTEAU DE PRAY
historic

Route de Chargé
Amboise
37400 Indre-et-Loire

Tel 00 33 2.47.57.23.67
Fax 00 33 2.47.57.32.50
Email chateau.depray@wanadoo.fr
Website http://praycastel.online.fr

Named after its owner in 1244, Geoffroy de Pray, this small château stands in a park above the Loire, outside Amboise. It is now an elegant hotel (managed by Graziella Laurenty; her husband, Ludovic, is chef), which has drawn a rave review. 'A beautiful old building, so interesting and full of heraldry. A comfortable bedroom, a good bathroom, good house-keeping, cosy atmosphere. The food was sensational, in an impressive timbered-ceiling dining room (lots of colourful shields on the beams).' The gourmet menu at €50 includes foie gras de canard with pear chutney; turbot with mushrooms and artichokes. Smoking is allowed in the restaurant, but cigar devotees are directed to a *caveau à cigare*. Concerts of classical music are sometimes held.

Open All year, except Christmas, 1st 3 weeks Jan. Restaurant closed Tues night/Wed, Thurs midday low season. **Rooms** 19 double. **Facilities** Tea room, restaurant. 5-hectare grounds: terrace, garden, heated swimming pool. **Location** 3 km E of Amboise, on D751, 20 km from Tours. **Credit cards** Amex, MasterCard, Visa. **Terms** Room €95–€170. Breakfast €11. D,B&B €99–€136 per person.

HÔTEL AGNÈS SOREL   value

4 quai Pasteur	*Tel* 00 33 2.47.93.04.37
Chinon	*Fax* 00 33 2.47.93.06.37
37500 Indre-et-Loire	*Email* info@agnes-sorel.com
	Website www.agnes-sorel.com

Named for a mistress of Charles VII (she was an enthusiastic cook), this 'sweet, unpretentious little place, astonishingly cheap' – in Chinon, 45 km south-west of Tours – makes a fine base for château-visiting. Owned and run by 'smilingly friendly' Catherine Raoust and her husband, it stands by the river Vienne, below the great castle. It is in two sections: 'Ours, separate from the main one, had a little terrace with tables, chairs and creepers, delightful in summer.' More praise: 'A warm welcome and much helpfulness. Our good-sized room had two narrow balconies overlooking the river. Inevitably it heard traffic; earplugs helped.' 'Our room across a side alley lacked a view, but had character to compensate.' 'Room service was charming, even on a wet night when Madame had to go out into the rain. Accommodation is homely rather than elegant. Our bathroom was fine and modern.' Breakfast (freshly squeezed orange juice, a generous plateful of croissants, etc), in a 'tastefully decorated high-ceilinged room', or in the bedroom, 'was nicely done'.

Open All year. **Rooms** 1 suite, 10 double. In 2 different houses. **Facilities** Reception, breakfast room. Terrace. Small garden. **Location** Central, between castle and river (rear rooms quietest). **Credit cards** MasterCard, Visa. **Terms** Room €45–€70, suite €92–€110. Breakfast €7.

DOMAINE DE LA TORTINIÈRE luxury

10 route de Ballan-Miré *Tel* 00 33 2.47.34.35.00
Les Gués de Veigné *Fax* 00 33 2.47.65.95.70
Montbazon *Email* domaine.tortiniere@wanadoo.fr
37250 Indre-et-Loire *Website* www.tortiniere.com

'A lovely hotel', enjoyed again by visitors. The owner/ managers, Anne and Xavier Olivereau, are the fourth generation of the family to run this handsome pepperpotted Second Empire mansion, set amid woods and lawns in a park. A luxurious Relais du Silence, it has glorious views over the valley of the Indre from its lovely dining terrace. Some suites are in the turrets, eight luxurious rooms are in recently converted stables. 'Our lovely large room had a deck with a beautiful view.' 'Ours was lushly furnished.' In the orangery restaurant, chef Freddy Lefebvre's menus are based on '*la richesse du terroir*' (pigeon, rabbit, beef, etc). One guest called his cooking 'complex, subtle, delicious', and found breakfast 'wonderful'. 'Very good service, especially at dinner.' 'The rowing boat was still there for guests to dabble in the slow waters of the Indre,' said a returning visitor, 'and the view across to the tower of Montbazon was as clear as ever.' There's an outdoor swimming pool, and Loire châteaux, Villandry, Chenonceaux, etc, are not far.

Open 1 Mar–20 Dec. Closed Sun evening 15 Nov–30 Mar. **Rooms** 9 suites, 20 double. **Facilities** Salon, bar, restaurant, terrace. **Location** 10 km S of Tours, 2 km N of Montbazon by N10 and D287. Parking. **Credit cards** MasterCard, Visa. **Terms** Room €98–€222, suite €278. Breakfast €14. D,B&B €113–€234 per person.

GERMANY

ALTENBURG
(Ryanair)

The airport is 58 km south of Leipzig and
just over 100 km from Dresden.

HOTEL KRELLER   value

Fischerstrasse 5
Freiberg
09599 Sachsen

Tel 00 49 3731 3 59 00
Fax 00 49 3731 2 32 19
Email kontakt@hotel-kreller.de
Website www.hotel-kreller.de

This small Saxon university city, between Altenburg and
Dresden, is famous for its 16th-century baroque Marienkirche
and its museums, and it makes a good base for exploring the
former mining centres and present-day makers of wooden
Christmas ornaments in the towns of the nearby Erzgebirge
mountains. In its centre, the Kreller family's old hotel offers
good-value lodging, says a visitor. 'It has a homelike character,
including in the restaurant, popular with locals. Breakfast is
excellent, even by German standards. Only reservation: the
owners' love affair with plastic plants, which are everywhere; I
breakfasted under a plastic palm tree.'

Open All year. **Rooms** 37. **Facilities** Lift. Lounge, bar, restaurant.
Beer garden. **Location** 49 km SW of Dresden. In historic centre,
at main post office, turn left at 1st street; hotel 50 m on left. Car
park. **Credit cards** All major cards accepted. **Terms** B&B: single
€50–€92, double €66–€87, suite €87–€107. Alc €16–€38.

HOTEL BÜLOW RESIDENZ   baroque

Rähnitzgasse 19
01097 Dresden

Tel 00 49 351 8 00 30
Fax 00 49 351 8 00 31 00
Email info@buelow-residenz.de
Website www.buelow-residenz.de

In a quiet street across the Elbe from the historic centre (all the sights are within walking distance), this yellow-fronted, 18th-century baroque mansion is now Horst and Monika Bülow's small luxury hotel (Relais & Châteaux), managed by Ralf Kutzner. 'Not cheap, but excellent', it was enjoyed by inspectors this year: 'Our large, attractive bedroom had modern furniture, a good bathroom, and the best, softest duvets ever.' Internet access is now available. In the smart *Caroussel* restaurant (*Michelin* star), the chef, Stefan Hermann, produces French and Swabian cuisine. 'Dinner was elegant in the modern manner, so many *amuse-bouches* and *petits fours*, we needed to order only two courses, and when we thought we had finished, a huge tray of chocolate truffles was brought. Breakfast was a wonderful buffet. We didn't see the owners, but the young staff were charming. Only caveat: the piped music was out of character.' There is an atmospheric vaulted cellar bar. Alfresco meals are served under trees in a leafy courtyard.

Open All year. Restaurant closed Sun/Mon. **Rooms** 5 suites, 24 double, 1 single. **Facilities** Lift. Salon, cellar bar, restaurant. Courtyard (meal service). **Location** Central. Parking 50 m. **Credit cards** All major cards accepted. **Terms** Room: single €120–€180, double €180–€220, suite €270–€410. Breakfast €17. D,B&B €60 added per person.

BERLIN

(Air Berlin, easyJet, Ryanair)

Air Berlin flies to Tegel, 8 km from the
city centre. EasyJet and Ryanair fly to Schönefeld,
18 km from the centre.

ART'OTEL BERLIN MITTE   designer

Wallstrasse 70–73   *Tel* 00 49 30 24 06 20
10179 Berlin   *Fax* 00 49 30 24 06 22 22
                    Email aobminfo@artotels.de
                    Website www.artotel.de

Built six years ago by Austrian architect Johanne Nalbach,
this designer hotel in historic and lively Berlin-Mitte,
'stunningly beautiful', is decorated with original pictures,
mainly by Georg Baselitz. 'Wonderful', 'brilliant' are recent
comments. 'All is calm elegance: white beds and curtains,
gentle colour in the fabrics.' On the top floor are large
rooms with a kitchenette, with views of floodlit spires. 'The
staff, mainly young, are efficient.' The extensive buffet
breakfast includes 'copious fruit salad, 12 types of tea'. It is
served in a glass-roofed atrium which links the modern hotel
to a 17th-century patrician building. A sister hotel, *art'otel city
centre west*, is filled with works by Andy Warhol.

Open All year. Restaurant closed midday, July/Aug, Sun/Mon.
Rooms 10 apartments, 4 suites, 82 double, 13 single. **Facilities**
Lift. Reception, 2 restaurants; dining terrace. **Location** SE side of
Berlin-Mitte. (U-Bahn: Märkisches Ufer) **Credit cards** All major
cards accepted. **Terms** B&B: single €108–€168, double
€138–€198, suite €138–€248. Alc from €22.

BLEIBTREU HOTEL   **funky**

Bleibtreustrasse 31   *Tel* 00 49 30 88 47 40
10707 Berlin   *Fax* 00 49 30 88 47 44 44
                                    Email info@bleibtreu.com
                                    Website www.bleibtreu.com

This 'funky' designer hotel was liked by inspectors for its
youthful feel and its position: 'It is in a street of attractive
shops, just off the Ku'Damm, yet so quiet we could sleep
with the windows open. It has some failings, eg, the water
was not always hot, and reception can be over-pressed, but
they are helpful; the food in the restaurant was excellent:
very good fish and vegetarian dishes, breakfast was good
too, nothing packaged.' A glass lift goes to the bedrooms:
'Ours had oatmeal-coloured fabrics, and a bathroom
dashingly tiled in shades of blue. A delicious apple was by
each bed.' The emphasis is on 'wellness': the food is organic,
and eco-friendly materials have been used throughout,
including organic paint. The remote-control switches in the
bedrooms may be confusing, but the 'supremely soft' beds
are admired. Snack meals are served in a deli.

Open All year. **Rooms** 60. **Facilities** Lift. Lobby, sitting area, deli,
coffee shop, bar restaurant. **Location** Central, off Ku'Damm, near
Savignyplatz. (U-Bahn: Savignyplatz) **Credit cards** All major cards
accepted. **Terms** Room: single €142–€222, double €152–€232.
Breakfast €15. Alc €25–€36.

HECKER'S HOTEL   modern

Grolmanstrasse 35   *Tel* 00 49 30 8 89 00
10623 Berlin   *Fax* 00 49 30 8 89 02 60
                                          Email info@heckers-hotel.de
                                       Website www.heckers-hotel.de

In a street between the Ku'Damm and the Savignyplatz, Hans-Joachim Weber's efficient and stylish hotel has a roof terrace and glamorous modern decor (lots of glass, ceiling lights, angular furniture). The new suites are notably glossy. 'One of the best hotels we have stayed in,' say recent guests. 'Excellent service, a spacious room.' Most bedrooms are large and bright, with a marble bathroom; some have a kitchenette. Some can get noise. The good buffet breakfast includes eggs and bacon, 'but tables a bit cramped'. The hotel's Mediterranean-style *Cassambalis* restaurant is much liked.

Open All year. **Rooms** 3 suites, 45 double, 21 single. **Facilities** Lift, ramps. Lobby, coffee shop, bar, restaurant; roof terrace. **Location** Central, between Ku'Damm and Savignyplatz; rear rooms quietest. (U-Bahn: Uhlandstrasse) **Credit cards** All major cards accepted. **Terms** Room: single €125–€210, double €150–€220, suite €300–€495. Breakfast €15. D,B&B €29 added per person.

COLOGNE
(German Wings)

The airport is 15 km south-east of the city.

HOTEL BUCHHOLZ   value

Kunibertsgasse 5
50668 Cologne

Tel 00 49 221 16 08 30
Fax 00 49 221 1 60 83 41
Email info@hotel-buchholz.de
Website www.hotel-buchholz.de

In a listed building (with peach façade and white awnings) just
north of the cathedral, the Welsh-born owner, Carole Ann
Buchholz (she is 'a mine of information'), runs this small B&B
hotel with her son, Sascha. It is 'friendly, comfortable, quiet,
very good value', say admirers, and the owners say that
children are warmly welcomed. Bedrooms have Lloyd Loom
furniture, a big sofa, free 24-hour room service. 'Our room
was large, modernised.' Some bathrooms and shower
rooms are small. Back rooms are quietest. 'Copious, varied
breakfast' in a pleasant, rustic-style room (yellow walls and
pine tables), next to the small bar.

Open 4 Jan–23 Dec. **Rooms** 3 suites, 9 double, 7 single.
Facilities Lift. TV room, bar, breakfast room; terrace. **Location**
Central, near station and cathedral. Airport transfer (€29). **Credit
cards** All major cards accepted. **Terms** B&B: single €63–€94,
double €84–€179, suite €115–€189.

HOTEL IM WASSERTURM   modern

Kaygasse 2   *Tel* 00 49 221 2 00 80
50676 Cologne   *Fax* 00 49 221 2 00 88 88
                                   Email info@hotel-im-wasserturm.de
                                   Website www.hotel-im-wasserturm.de

A 19th-century water tower, a sturdy brick cylinder, has been turned into this luxury hotel with ultra-modern decor. It stands in large grounds (with chairs, tables and parasols in summer) in a residential area, barely a kilometre from the *Dom*. It is 'full of excellent modern art', as befits this German modern-art capital. Recent visitors 'were made most welcome'. An eight-room conference centre and a restaurant in the grounds have recently been added. Some readers dislike the 'austere design', but others think it 'magnificent' and imaginative: 'Our wedge-shaped junior suite was a fine creation: a single orchid adorned each black wood table.' But the designer style may not always be practical: 'The bath was in a black hole (no light to read by). And no stand for our suitcase.' The two-level suites have a spiral staircase. In the rooftop restaurant, the chef, Hendrik Otto, serves 'French food with a Mediterranean twist'. 'An excellent candlelit dinner; a superb wine list; a huge buffet breakfast.' Good snacks in *Harry's Lounge* (with pianist).

Open All year. **Rooms** 34 suites, 44 double, 10 single. **Facilities** Lift. Lounge, piano bar, 2 restaurants; roof terrace. **Location** Central, 1.5 km SW of cathedral. Underground garage. **Credit cards** All major cards accepted. **Terms** Room: single €180–€265, double €210–€335, suite €240–€1680. Breakfast €18. Set lunch €30, dinner €48; full alc €55.

DÜSSELDORF
(Air Berlin, Ryanair)

Air Berlin flies to Düsseldorf international airport, close to the city. Ryanair flies to Niederrhein, some 70 km north-west. This hotel is within reasonable distance of both.

SCHLOSS HUGENPOET · luxury

August-Thyssen-Strasse 51	*Tel* 00 49 2054 1 20 40
Essen-Kettwig	*Fax* 00 49 2054 12 04 50
45219 Nordrhein-Westfalen	*Email* info@hugenpoet.de
	Website www.hugenpoet.de

This moated 17th-century castle (Relais & Châteaux) stands amid woods in a posh little town outside Essen, near the river Ruhr. The owner is Michael Lübbert. 'Affable and impressive, much in evidence, he speaks perfect English,' says an inspector. He has appointed a new chef, Erika Bergheim, for the *Nesselrode* gourmet restaurant (a visitor found her cooking 'sophisticated, well presented, quite *nouvelle*, served by suave young men'). And he has opened an informal bistro/*Weinkeller, Hügenpöttchen*. Meals, including the good buffet breakfast, can be taken on the terrace in fine weather. The bedrooms are 'sumptuous', though some are 'smallish'; those on the second floor have Asian antiques.

Open All year. *Nesselrode* closed Tues. **Rooms** 5 suites, 14 double, 6 single. **Facilities** Lift, ramps. Lobby, salon, restaurant, bistro. **Location** 11 km SW of Essen. Ratingen-Breitscheid exit at A3/A52 interchange, B227 towards Velbert, then Essen-Kettwig. **Credit cards** All major cards accepted. **Terms** B&B: single €189, double €225–€270, suite €350–€490. Set meals: bistro €28–€42; *Nesselrode* €69–€89.

FRANKFURT/HAHN
(Ryanair)

Ryanair flies to Hahn, 110 km from Frankfurt.
Here we suggest a city hotel, and two hotels
on the Mosel river, closer to the airport.

HOTEL WESTEND   old-world

Westendstrasse 15
Frankfurt am Main
60325 Hessen

Tel 00 49 69 78 98 81 80
Fax 00 49 69 74 53 96
Email hotel_westend@t-online.de
Website www.hotelwestend.com

A listed building of character, with a pleasant garden where drinks can be served, the Mayer family's small, personal B&B hotel is unusual for central Frankfurt with its big, brash modern ones. It is quite near the skyscrapers, but in a quiet, mainly residential district. Managed 'attentively' by Zafer Morgan, it offers old-world service by discreet men in black suits. The 'tasteful decor' includes antiques, old paintings, brass chandeliers and oriental rugs: but there's no lift, and many stairs. Bedrooms have 'exquisite bedlinen' and Internet access. Breakfast, 'ample and good' with 'terrific coffee', is served in the lounges or on the terrace.

Open All year, except 23 Dec–5 Jan. **Rooms** 1 suite, 11 double, 8 single. **Facilities** 3 lounges (1 with TV). Garden: terrace. **Location** Central, off Mainzer Landstrasse between Messe fairgrounds and station. Parking. **Credit cards** All major cards accepted. **Terms** B&B: single €50–€160, double €100–€220, suite €170–€380.

LILLER'S HISTORISCHE SCHLOSSMÜHLE   folksy

An der Landstrasse 190   *Tel* 00 49 6543 40 41
Horbruch im Hunsrück   *Fax* 00 49 6543 31 78
55483 Rheinland-Pfalz   *Email* info@historische-schlossmuehle.de

On the Hunsrück plateau, near Bernkastel and close to Hahn airport, this 17th-century mill house is now an unusual hotel, run in folksy style. Recent visitors wrote of the 'genuine welcome', and the 'delightful courtesy' of the hosts, Anne and Rüdiger Liller. 'At the door is a fountain decorated with a frog prince and a princess'; everywhere are pictures, ornaments, knick-knacks (many are for sale). Rooms in the main house (some open on to a little patio with tables and chairs) are comfortable, if small and crowded with furniture and ornaments. One couple, both under five foot six, 'had difficulty getting around the clutter without sending things flying', but 'we enjoyed our stay immensely'. The food is 'excellent, in the modern German style that has the virtues of *nouvelle cuisine* but nothing to do with small portions'. The huge old mill wheel still turns in a stream by the dining room. Some bedrooms are in a cottage annexe. 'First-class breakfast.'

Open 16 Jan–31 Dec. Restaurant closed Mon. **Rooms** 2 suites, 16 double. 8 in annexe. **Facilities** Lounge, library, breakfast room, restaurant. Large garden. **Location** Horbruch is 12 km SE of Bernkastel-Kues. Hotel (signposted) is just outside village. **Credit cards** MasterCard, Visa. **Terms** B&B: double €115–€160, suite €172. Set lunch €30, dinner €38; full alc €50.

JUGENDSTIL HOTEL BELLEVUE   Art Nouveau

Am Moselufer
Traben-Trarbach
56841 Rheinland-Pfalz

Tel 00 49 6541 70 30
Fax 00 49 6541 70 34 00
Email info@bellevue-hotel.de
Website www.bellevue-hotel.de

Just 20 km from Hahn international airport, Matthias Ganter's recently restored, authentic *Jugendstil* building (Romantik Hotels) has a splendid situation by the river banks, on the edge of this leading Mosel wine town. Its 'stunning interiors' have delighted visitors. So did 'taking breakfast in the elegant Art Nouveau dining room'. Service is found 'impeccable', and 'having aperitifs and dinner on the river terrace was a delight. Our spacious corner room had a sitting area in the turret, and a view up and down the river.' Bedrooms are modern and comfortable; some suites are in an annexe. Steffen Schubotz, the chef, serves 'dinners of a high standard', with 'huge puddings'. To help work this off, the fitness and beauty facilities have been much enlarged.

Open All year. **Rooms** 12 suites, 23 double, 2 single. 24 apartments in annexe (100 m). **Facilities** Lift. Salon, bar, restaurant; indoor swimming pool. Terrace. **Location** 150 m from centre. 63 km NE of Trier. **Credit cards** All major cards accepted. **Terms** B&B: single €71–€89, double €119–€169, suite €149–€198; D,B&B €22.50 added per person. Min. 2-night stay weekends.

FRIEDRICHSHAFEN
(Ryanair)

The airport is 3 km north of Lake Constance.

GASTHOF ZUM BÄREN   romantic

Marktplatz 11   *Tel* 00 49 7532 4 32 20
Meersburg   *Fax* 00 49 7532 43 22 44
88709 Baden-Württemberg *Email* gasthofzumbaeren@t-online.de
                          Website www.meersburg.de/baeren

'It was a delight,' say recent visitors to this handsome old building on the small market square of the prettiest town on Lake Constance. An inn since 1605, it is now a 'romantic and charming hotel', run for five generations by the Gilowsky family – today by Michael Gilowsky, whose cooking of zander fresh from the lake is much enjoyed. 'Rustic, warm and comfortable', it has antiques, steep creaking stairways (no lift), and carvings and flowerpots on its picturesque corner tower, where the best bedrooms have an alcove from which you can watch the lively scene below. Each room is different: 'Ours was a romantic ensemble of celadon-green antiques. The smart modern bathroom was small; others are larger. Breakfast was a nice buffet.'

Open 15 Mar–15 Nov. Restaurant closed Mon. **Rooms** 17 double, 3 single. **Facilities** Restaurant. **Location** Central, in pedestrian zone (free car access for hotel guests). **Credit cards** None accepted. **Terms** B&B: single €48, double €78–€104; D,B&B €18 added per person.

HAMBURG/LÜBECK
(Ryanair)

Ryanair flies to Lübeck airport,
80 km north-east of Hamburg.

GARDEN HOTELS
city chic

Magdalenenstrasse 60
Hamburg
20148 Hamburg

Tel 00 49 40 41 40 40
Fax 00 49 40 4 14 04 20
Email garden@garden-hotels.de
Website www.garden-hotels.de

This modern hotel consists of three houses, surrounded by trees and gardens, in a quiet street. It is in the trendy Pöseldorf district, on the west bank of the Aussenalster lake, a haunt of the media. Within easy reach are restaurants and shops. 'Attractively decorated, hung with modern pictures, it has a certain chic,' said visitors. 'Our comfortable room had two sofas, a spacious bathroom. Polite service.' The 'good breakfast', available all day, is served in a conservatory in the main house or, in summer, on the bedroom balconies or in the pleasant gardens.

Open All year. **Rooms** 6 apartments with kitchenette, 2 suites, 37 double, 20 single. In 3 buildings. **Facilities** Lifts. Breakfast conservatory; conference room. Small gardens. **Location** W side of Aussenalster lake, 3 km N of centre. Parking. (U-Bahn: Hallerstrasse) **Credit cards** All major cards accepted. **Terms** Room: single €125–€205, double €145–€280. Breakfast €9–€11.

KARLSRUHE/BADEN
(Ryanair)

The airport is near to historic Baden-Baden,
close to the French border.

HOTEL AM MARKT   **budget**

Marktplatz 18	*Tel* 00 49 7221 2 70 40
Baden-Baden	*Fax* 00 49 7221 27 04 44
76530 Baden-Württemberg	

Email info@hotel-am-markt-baden.de
Website www.hotel-am-markt-baden.de

An unlikely find in the heart of posh Baden-Baden, this unassuming hostelry, trim and pink-fronted, stands in the old part of town near the cathedral, and 400 metres from the baths. Owned and run since 1950 by the Bogner family, it is thought 'good value and well run', 'excellent in all ways'. It is 'nicely decorated', and has 'very good breakfasts' and 'good service'. Plentiful, freshly cooked dishes are served to residents from a limited menu (but only until 7.30 pm). They are taken in the *Stübe*, or on a pleasant terrace. Some bedrooms are reached only by stairs.

Open All year. Dining room closed midday and to non-residents. **Rooms** 12 double, 13 single. 13 with bath and/or shower, 2 with WC. **Facilities** 2 lounges with TV, dining room. Small terrace. **Location** Central. In pedestrian zone: follow blue sign: *Thermen/Rathaus*. Free parking up the hill. **Credit cards** All major cards accepted. **Terms** B&B: single €31–€50, double €60–€80. Set dinner €9–€16.

HOTEL HEILIGENSTEIN   welcoming

Heiligensteinstrasse 19a	*Tel* 00 49 7223 9 61 40
Neuweier	*Fax* 00 49 7223 96 14 50
76534 Baden-Württemberg	*Email* gast@hotel-heiligenstein.de
	Website www.hotel-heiligenstein.de

'Very pleasant with attractive rooms and a delicious buffet breakfast', this spruce, chalet-style hotel stands near vineyards, in a big wine village south-west of Baden-Baden. 'Our welcome was warm and friendly, the room comfortable and well furnished,' was another comment. Owned by Barbara Beck and managed by Bettina Fundinger, it has a fire in the lounge bar, and a sunny terrace for drinks and coffee. The evening meal can be a *Vesper* (snack), or you can take the menu of the day. 'Delicious local wines.' Some bedrooms are large, with massive wood furnishings and a balcony – 'splendid views' – and 'quiet, except for birdsong'. 'Lots of kitsch, much of it for sale.'

Open Apr–Dec, except Christmas. Restaurant closed Tues. **Rooms** 3 suites, 18 double, 9 single. **Facilities** Lift. Lobby, TV room, bar, restaurant; billiard room. Terrace. Garden. **Location** Edge of village. 10 km SW of Baden-Baden, 7 km NE of Bühl. Parking. **Credit cards** MasterCard, Visa. **Terms** B&B: single €48–€62, double €87–€104, suite €140–€160; D,B&B €24 added per person.

MÖNCHS WALDHOTEL   hunting lodge

Kapfenhardt Mühle
Unterreichenbach
75399 Baden-Württemberg

Tel 00 49 7235 79 00
Fax 00 49 7235 79 01 90

Email moenchs.waldhotel@t-online.de
Website moenchs-waldhotel.de

On the north-east edge of the Black Forest, near the pretty town of Calw – 40 km east of Baden-Baden – Stefan Mönch's fairly smart hotel is a timbered chalet-type building in traditional style, with panelled wooden ceilings. It is liked for the 'excellent friendly welcome' and 'hunting-lodge atmosphere'. 'It has 65 bedrooms, yet did not feel like a big hotel,' say admirers. One reader told of 'a huge, comfortable family room; superb, attractive indoor pool and spa' (with two large saunas, plunge pool, gentle music). 'Our balcony with loungers looked over the forest. The restaurant was fine'; 'enormous portions of pleasant, well-prepared food': many local dishes (eg, Maultaschen; venison goulash with Spätzle) are on the extensive menu. 'Wonderful buffet breakfast.' 'Fruit crumble at tea was exceptional, but no Black Forest gâteau.' You can eat on the terrace in summer.

Open All year, except Christmas. **Rooms** 1 suite, 36 double, 29 single. **Facilities** Lift. Lounge, TV room, bar, restaurant; conservatory. Garden. **Location** 14 km N of Calw, at Kapfenhardt. Parking. **Credit cards** All major cards accepted. **Terms** B&B €48.50–€80; D,B&B €20 added per person.

MUNICH
(easyJet)

The airport is 28 km north-east of the city.

BRAUEREIGASTHOF-HOTEL AYING   intoxicating

Zornedingerstrasse 2
Aying
85653 Bavaria

Tel 00 49 8095 9 06 50
Fax 00 49 8095 90 65 66
Email brauereigasthof@ayinger-bier.de
Website www.ayinger-bier.de

Lovers of beer should be in their element at this large, old, creeper-covered Bavarian inn, 14th-century in origin. In their Ayinger brewery next door, rated 'Best Small Brewery' at the World Beer Championships in Chicago for five years running, the Inselkammer family produces 13 different beers: the smell of malt and hops is never far away. For eating, there is a restaurant in three rooms, one the historic *Kegelbahn*, and a large beer garden across the street. The 'very good' cooking of chef Josef Rampl, served in large portions, is a mix of Bavarian and more sophisticated (*Michelin Bib Gourmand*). 'Beer and atmosphere both intoxicating,' was one recent comment. Some bedrooms have Bavarian hand-painted furniture. Breakfast, a varied buffet, has 'lashings of good coffee'.

Open All year, except 24 Dec. **Rooms** 25 double, 9 single. **Facilities** Lift. 3 dining rooms; lobby. Garden: courtyard. **Location** Central (quiet at night). 25 km SE of Munich. Large car park. **Credit cards** All major cards accepted. **Terms** B&B: single €95–€180, double €135–€180. Set lunch €15, dinner €30; full alc €31.

HOTEL MARIENBAD   down to earth

Barerstrasse 11   *Tel* 00 49 89 59 55 85
Munich   *Fax* 00 49 89 59 82 38
80333 Munich   *Email* info@hotelmarienbad.de
                              Website www.hotelmarienbad.de

Rilke and Mahler have stayed in this solid red-roofed mansion, now the Grüner family's down-to-earth B&B hotel. Near the Alte Pinakothek and other major museums, it is in a business area but fairly quiet. Its devotees find it 'pleasant and unpretentious'. 'Service is friendly, breakfast is good, and prices are moderate.' 'The helpful owners and their staff always have interesting titbits of gossip about Munich.' Most rooms are good sized, 'if a bit old-fashioned': they have sturdy pine furniture, plenty of cupboard space, a bright bathroom. On the top floor is a flat with kitchen and splendid views – 'ideal for a longish stay'.

Open All year, except Christmas/New Year. **Rooms** 2 suites, 17 double, 11 single. **Facilities** Lift. Breakfast room/lounge; terrace. **Location** 1 km NW of centre, near Alte Pinakothek. Free private parking. (U-Bahn: Karlsplatz) **Credit cards** None accepted. **Terms** B&B: single €45–€85, double €105–€115, suite €135.

HUNGARY

BUDAPEST
(easyJet, Sky Europe)

The airport is 16 km south-east of the city.

ART'OTEL
hip

Bem Rakpart 16–19
1011 Budapest

Tel 00 36 1 487 9487
Fax 00 36 1 487 9488
Email budapest@artotel.hu
Website www.artotel.hu

The managers describe it as a 'hip lifestyle hotel'. A visitor called it 'really nice, with very helpful English-speaking staff'. Four restored 18th-century baroque houses have been integrated to create this designer hotel on the Danube embankment, opposite the lovely Parliament building. The castle district is an easy walk away. The decor is 'modern and cheerful' (much red and grey). Six hundred works by a minimalist American artist, Donald Sultan, fill the building: he also designed the upholstery and the crockery. Most bedrooms face the river but are quiet. The 'very good' restaurant serves Hungarian and international food. Breakfast is a huge hot and cold buffet.

Open All year. **Rooms** 9 suites, 147 double, 8 single. **Facilities** Lift, ramps. Lobby, lounge/breakfast room, café, restaurant. Terrace. **Location** On Danube, in Buda, facing Chain Bridge. Garage. (Metro: Batthyány Sq) **Credit cards** All major cards accepted. **Terms** B&B: single €99–€198, double €99–€218, suite €198–€298; D,B&B double €129–€248.

HOTEL ASTRA VENDÉGHÁZ   value

Vám utca 6
1011 Budapest

Tel 00 36 1 214 1906
Fax 00 36 1 214 1907
Email hotelastra@euroweb.hu
Website www.hotelastra.hu

Down a side street below the fascinating, if touristy, castle district of Buda, this stylish little B&B, 'quiet, clean, comfortable and convenient', managed by Tamás Érsek, is a white building, three centuries old. It has tall airy public rooms with period furnishings, and a cellar bar. Recently renovated, and 'a bargain at the price', it is much praised. 'I loved it. Wonderfully quiet. My spacious room, with lovely warm bathroom, led on to the geranium-covered courtyard. It was like having my own little house.' 'Charming, with helpful staff.' 'Well decorated. Suites particularly good value' (they have 'lavish furniture and equipment, a good modern bathroom'). One couple's room was small, with the bathroom opposite (a late booking). The buffet breakfast, in a 'pleasant room', is 'adequate, if not startling'. Good Hungarian eating nearby: *À la Carte* is recommended.

Open All year. **Rooms** 3 suites, 8 double. **Facilities** Lounge, cellar bar with snooker; breakfast room. **Location** In Buda, just N of castle. **Credit cards** None accepted. **Terms** B&B: single €80–€90, double €95–€105, suite €125–€135.

CITY HOTEL PILVAX   value

Pilvax köz 1–3   *Tel* 00 36 1 266 7660
1052 Budapest   *Fax* 00 36 1 317 6396
                                  Email pilvax@taverna.hu
                                  Website www.taverna.hu

A medium-priced hotel, part of the small Taverna chain, in the business district of Pest. It occupies the lower floors of a 1930s-style block, on a traffic-free side street, near the city's main shopping street (Váci utca). It is on the site of the former Pilvax coffee house, where the Hungarian independence movement of 1848 began (display cases in the dining room contain memorabilia, with explanations in Hungarian). The decor is 'rather 1980s', but there is now air-conditioning. 'Rooms vary in size: ours was an unusual trapezoid shape, but very comfortable,' say returning visitors. 'Rooms at the back may be even quieter, but perhaps a bit gloomy. Housekeeping was excellent, and staff were very friendly and efficient: most spoke English.' Breakfast, in the panelled restaurant, is 'the usual Hungarian cold buffet, plus one hot dish on offer'. The *Pilvax* restaurant 'offers good food and reasonable value': in summer, it has tables and chairs on a terrace, under a canopy. The Danube is five minutes' walk away.

Open All year. Restaurant closed 24 Dec. **Rooms** 4 triple, 26 double, 2 single. **Facilities** Lounge, bar, restaurant. **Location** Central, in Pest. Airport shuttle. (Metro: Ferenciek er) **Credit cards** All major cards accepted. **Terms** B&B: single €55–€75, double €75–€99. Set lunch €10, dinner €12; full alc €14.

HOTEL GELLÉRT   grandeur

Szent Gellért tér 1   *Tel* 00 36 1 889 5500
1111 Budapest   *Fax* 00 36 1 889 5505
                    Email gellert.reservation@danubiusgroup.com
                    Website www.danubiusgroup.com/gellert

On the Buda bank of the Danube, this Art Nouveau white palace (1918) has a lavish decor: marbled halls, stained-glass windows, wrought ironwork and a splendid stairway. Reviews can be mixed, but a regular visitor writes: 'The anonymous chain or fashionable boutique hotels nearby may offer more modern comforts, but only at the *Gellért* will one feel truly at home in Budapest. It may have seen better days, but it is probably the atmosphere of decaying grandeur that makes it so attractive to foreign visitors.' The best, spacious front bedrooms, with old-fashioned furniture and big windows, face the river. Some other rooms can be 'poky'. At the buffet breakfast, in two hill/river-facing rooms, the young staff are 'eager if sometimes a bit disorganised'. The coffee shop is a local meeting place. In the restaurant, local dishes are served by 'attentive' waiters; folk dancers sometimes perform. 'The jewel in the crown is the thermal baths', separately managed, often crowded. Hotel guests have special robes and access via a lift.

Open All year. **Rooms** 13 suites, 129 double, 92 single. **Facilities** Lounges, bar, brasserie, café, restaurant; beauty parlour; thermal baths. Garden: terraces, swimming pool. **Location** 3 km from centre (foot of Gellért hill). **Credit cards** All major cards accepted. **Terms** B&B: single €75–€180, double €190–€240, suite €270–€300.

IRELAND

CORK
(bmibaby, FlyBE, Ryanair)

The airport is just south of Ireland's second city.

BAYVIEW HOTEL   *sea views*

Ballycotton
Co. Cork

Tel 00 353 21-464 6746
Fax 00 353 21-464 6075
Email info@bayviewhotel.net
Website www.bayviewhotel.net

John and Carmel O'Brien's long, low and white holiday hotel is much liked by guests. 'The food was delicious, the views were spectacular,' says a visitor. 'Gorgeous.' It stands in its own grounds on the edge of the cliffs, above this 'elongated' fishing village. From its pretty terraced garden, steps lead down to the sea. All bedrooms are spacious and have sea views; some have small balconies. 'We were indulged by a competent and willing staff. The dining room was superbly run, with sophistication. Breakfasts were good, with a wonderful display of fruit.' Others enjoyed the flowers, the old paintings, and the peace.

Open I Mar–26 Oct. **Rooms** 35 double. **Facilities** Lift. 2 lounges, bar, restaurant. **Location** 20 miles SE of Cork. Take N25 to Midleton, turn right on to B629 to Ballycotton. Bayview in village centre, near harbour. **Credit cards** All major cards accepted. **Terms** B&B: single €111–€129, double €158–€229. Set lunch €24, dinner €45.

BALLYMALOE HOUSE   favourite

Shanagarry
Co. Cork

Tel 00 353 21-465 2531
Fax 00 353 21-465 2021
Email res@ballymaloe.ie
Website www.ballymaloe.com

'Excellent'; 'magical'; 'marvellous'; 'food throughout our longish stay was always superb' – continuing praise for a famous hotel/restaurant. Headed by the veteran Myrtle Allen, it is a true family enterprise: one daughter-in-law, Hazel, is manager; head chef is Rory O'Connell, brother of another daughter-in-law, Darina, the well-known cookery writer who runs the Ballymaloe Cookery School. 'We arrived late but had a warm welcome,' says a recent visitor. 'Our comfortable room in a new wing had French doors on to the attractive garden, with our own sitting area. The drawing room was always cosy. Here, over excellent sherry, our dinner order was taken in a very personal way, often by a member of the family. All service was cheerful and efficient.' This backs an earlier inspector's report: 'Such a happy atmosphere. It is like a cultured private home. The food is delicious and clever: wonderful turbot in champagne sauce; stunning cheeseboard; superb chocolates with coffee. Excellent breads. Breakfast had a very good marmalade and kippers.'

Open All year, except 22–26 Dec. **Rooms** 30 double, 3 single. **Facilities** Drawing room, 2 small sitting rooms, conservatory, 5 dining rooms. **Location** From Cork airport: N25 ring road towards Rosslare; at Midleton, turn S to Cloyne. Hotel on L35, 2 miles E of Cloyne. **Credit cards** All major cards accepted. **Terms** B&B: single €112.50–€167.50, double €195–€291. Set dinner €55.50.

GLENALLY HOUSE   excellent food

Youghal   *Tel/Fax* 00 353 24-91623
Co. Cork   *Email* enquiries@glenally.com
                                    Website www.glenally.com

Fred and Herta Rigney (he a Dubliner, she German by birth)
run this 'delightful' guest house, just outside a small market
town at the mouth of the Blackwater river. Our inspector
reports: 'Bought by the Rigneys in a run-down state, this late
Georgian house has been beautifully restored. Daring
combinations of textures and colours go wonderfully with
old furniture, modern light fittings. All bedrooms are large,
attractive, well lit, but with different colour schemes and
furnishings. The Rigneys are wonderfully gracious, also chatty.
Both are excellent cooks [members of the Slow Food move-
ment]. On the four-course no-choice menu (dinner must be
ordered in advance), we enjoyed delicious vegetable risotto;
roast lamb; excellent Irish cheeseboard; lovely rhubarb fool.
Dining is communal: no wine licence; bring your own.
Breakfast is a treat with fresh orange juice, porridge with
local honey, pancakes with baked bananas and maple syrup,
then cooked Irish with the famous Clonakilty black pudding.
Nothing pre-packed; and the hotel is non-smoking.' Another
visitor raved about the 'serious unpretentious cooking'.

Open Mar–end Dec. **Rooms** 4 double. No telephone. **Facilities**
Sitting room, breakfast room, dining room. **Location** Take N25
east from Cork. Over roundabout just E of Youghal, pass Esso
station. After 150 yds, left into small lane, after 50 yds turn right.
'Owners will fax sketch map.' **Credit cards** MasterCard, Visa.
Terms B&B: single €60–€75, double €100–€120. Set dinner €40.

ROCK COTTAGE   award-winning

Barnatonicane   *Tel/Fax* 00 353 28-35538
Schull   *Email* rockcottage@eircom.net
Co. Cork   *Website* www.mizen.net/rockcottage

Barbara Klötzer, from Germany, won the *Good Hotel Guide*'s César award in 2004 as the gracious host of Irish guest house of the year. 'We had a lovely stay,' said an inspector, enthusing over the three-bedroom Georgian hunting lodge in a secluded position near Dunmanus Bay, north-west of the lively holiday village of Schull. 'The setting is delightful, among grassy hillocks, mature trees, lambs in the fields, white ducks on parade, views of the sea, a well-kept garden. The rather stark black-and-white exterior belies the charm and elegant comfort within – tasteful decor, interesting and attractive furnishings, pictures, ornaments and flowers. The comfortable bedrooms have stunning outlooks, good lighting and bathrooms, interesting books. After drinks and *amuse-gueules* by the drawing room fire, the set dinner [served at 7.30 pm] was excellent. Breakfast, in the bright dining room, included fresh orange juice, cereal, scrambled egg with chives, good local black pudding, a gorgeous platter of fruit. I could not fault this place.'

Open All year. **Rooms** 2 family, 1 double. Also 1 self-catering cottage. **Facilities** Lounge, dining room. 7-hectare grounds. **Location** Take N71 south-west from Cork. At Ballydehob turn left on to R952. At Toormore, turn right on to R591 towards Durrus. B&B signpost on left, after 1½ miles. **Credit cards** MasterCard, Visa. **Terms** (*not VAT-rated*) B&B: single €60–€70, double €90–€110. Set dinner €35.

DUBLIN

(bmibaby, FlyBE, MyTravelLite, Ryanair)

The airport is on the M1, north of the
junction with the M50 ring road.

ASHBROOK HOUSE   value

River Road, Ashtown   *Tel/Fax* 00 353 1-838 5660
Castleknock, Dublin 15

'Secluded and quiet, like being in the country', yet only 15
minutes' drive from the city centre and the airport, Eve and
Stan Mitchell's beautiful Georgian house is now this stylish
B&B. 'It was like being welcomed into Mrs Mitchell's lovely
home,' says an enthusiastic visitor. 'Large bedroom and
bathroom, comfortable bed, lovely colours everywhere.'
The 'excellent breakfast', with attractive pottery, is served in
an 'elegant' room. There is a big walled garden with a grass
tennis court. 'Excellent transport to the centre', and plenty
of pubs nearby.

Open 2 Jan–20 Dec. **Rooms** 4 double. **Facilities** TV room,
breakfast room. Large garden. **Location** NW of centre, near
Phoenix Park and ring road to airport. **Restriction** No smoking.
Credit cards MasterCard, Visa. **Terms** B&B: single €60, double
€90.

ANGLESEA TOWN HOUSE   welcoming

63 Anglesea Road   *Tel* 00 353 1-668 3877
Ballsbridge, Dublin 4   *Fax* 00 353 1-668 3461

Helen Kirrane's 'luxurious B&B', 'lovely, friendly', 'is so superior it does not assert its identity externally': it is in a handsome Edwardian house on a busy road (quiet at night) in residential Ballsbridge. Many buses pass the door or the end of the road. A visitor reports: 'Hospitable; a good welcome from Mrs Kirrane and the continental staff in the beautiful, airy, atrium-style breakfast room.' Breakfast is 'huge and complicated'. 'Do not miss the warm compote of fruits which arrives about a third of the way through; fish or kedgeree are alternatives to the usual hot dishes.' There is also a selection of home-baked cakes, scones and tarts. The house is 'in superb condition, with period furniture, family photos', but one guest thought it 'a bit rule-bound'. Bedrooms vary. 'Ours was enormous: warm and comfortable bed; bathrobes and hair dryer, but rather bijou shower/loo room.' A single bedroom at the back was 'feminine, with salmon walls and silk taffeta curtains, embroidered white linen'.

Open All year, except Christmas/New Year. **Rooms** 7 double. **Facilities** Drawing room, breakfast room. **Location** 2 miles SE of centre, reached by buses, or by DART railway 650 yds away. **Restriction** No smoking. **Credit cards** Amex, MasterCard, Visa. **Terms** B&B: single €70, double €130.

KERRY
(Ryanair)

The airport is 9 miles from Killarney and
11 miles from Tralee.

GREENMOUNT HOUSE   charm

John Street	*Tel* 00 353 66-915 1414
Gortonora	*Fax* 00 353 66-915 1974
Dingle	*Email* greenmounthouse@aircom.net
Co. Kerry	

Dingle, an old fishing port, is now 'a very popular, buzzing town, even in April'. Here, Mary and John Curran have turned their family home above the town into a charming small B&B hotel, painted yellow. Its award-winning breakfasts are served in a long conservatory facing the hills and Dingle Bay. 'They are outstanding,' says an inspector: 'an array of freshly cut fruits in nice dishes; a cheeseboard with grapes; many breads; perfect lamb's liver; good scrambled egg with smoked salmon, leaf tea.' The red-walled sitting room has lots of books and an open fire. The luxury bedrooms, some 'with oodles of space', some 'a little cramped', all 'very neat and pristine', are in a separate block.

Open All year, except 10–27 Dec. **Rooms** 7 junior suites, 5 double. **Facilities** 2 lounges (1 with TV), reading room, breakfast room. **Location** From airport, take N22 to Tralee, turn left on N86 to Dingle (31 miles). 2nd right turn after entering Dingle; house on left. **Restrictions** No smoking. **Credit cards** MasterCard, Visa. **Terms** B&B: single €55–€85, double €90–€140.

CARAGH LODGE
lakeside

Caragh Lake	*Tel* 00 353 66-976 9115
Killorglin	*Fax* 00 353 66-976 9316
Co. Kerry	*Email* caraghl@iol.ie
	Website www.caraghlodge.com

'Mary Gaunt is a delight, she has made her Victorian fishing lodge a haven of comfort.' Praise for this low white house by the shore of Caragh Lake, set in seven acres of 'incredibly beautiful' gardens with rare trees and shrubs, and with views of the high Macgillicuddy's Reeks. 'When we drove up to the front door, her charming and superbly efficient South African assistant stepped forward to greet us by name. Pre-dinner drinks were served in the comfortable lounges where a fire is lit each evening, followed by superb food in an elegant room. The cuisine is 'French based with modern twists'. Breads are home-made. Breakfasts were 'very good, with an excellent variety of delicious fruits', also smoked salmon and scrambled eggs. Some rooms are in a garden wing, amid azaleas, camellias and magnolias: 'spacious, finely furnished, with a marvellous view and a large bathroom'. Those by the front courtyard were found 'adequate, trying to be elegant, but rather dark, with no view'.

Open 22 Apr–17 Oct. Lunch not served. **Rooms** 1 suite, 13 double, 1 single. Some in 2 annexes. No TV. **Facilities** 2 lounges, dining room. **Location** From airport take R561 to Castlemaine. Left on to N70 through Killorglin towards Glenbeigh; take road signposted *Caragh Lodge* 1 mile. Left at lake, lodge on right. **Credit cards** All major cards accepted. **Terms** B&B: single €130, double €180–€230, suite €325. Dinner €35–€45.

KNOCK
(bmibaby, MyTravelLite, Ryanair)

The airport is south of Charlestown,
Co. Mayo, midway between Galway and Sligo.

NEWPORT HOUSE   **luxury**

Newport   *Tel* 00 353 98-41222
Co. Mayo   *Fax* 00 353 98-41613
Email info@newporthouse.ie
Website www.relaischateaux.com/newport

Facing out towards Achill Island, this handsome, creeper-covered Georgian mansion stands in a much-visited village on lovely Clew Bay, amid fine scenery. It is owned and run by Thelma and Kieran Thompson, who offer 'great hospitality'; one recent guest called it 'marvellous'. It is a Relais & Châteaux member, but has an 'unstuffy atmosphere' and friendly service. The 'splendid' public rooms have fine plasterwork, chandeliers, 'cheerful fires burning'. The wine list is 'astonishing' and the gourmet menu was thought 'outstanding value'. Staff have been called 'wonderful'; and bedrooms 'gloriously old-fashioned' (some have a four-poster; some are suitable for a family). You can have eggs Benedict for breakfast, but there is no buffet, and service might be slow.

Open Mid-Mar–early Oct. **Rooms** 16 double, 2 single. 5 in courtyard. **Facilities** Drawing room, sitting room, bar, restaurant. 8-hectare grounds: walled garden. **Location** From Charlestown take N5 to Westport (35 miles). Newport is 7 miles north. **Credit cards** All major cards accepted. **Terms** B&B: single €129–€163, double €208–€276. Set dinner €50.

CROMLEACH LODGE   favourite

Castlebaldwin, via Boyle
Co. Sligo

Tel 00 353 71-916 5155
Fax 00 353 71-916 5455
Email info@cromleach.com
Website www.cromleach.com

Set on a low hillside above Lough Arrow, with views over lake and mountains from all bedrooms, Moira and Christy Tighe's small, sophisticated and warmly personal hotel is a striking modern building, glass fronted, grey gabled. A family operation with two sons actively involved, it has long been one of the most appreciated Irish rural retreats: the 'supreme comfort', the food and wines were lauded again recently. Mrs Tighe, a self-taught cook, won the Irish Chef of the Year award in 2000: she offers modern Irish cuisine 'with light sauces, intense flavours'. It does not come cheaply, but is much admired: a 'highly inventive' six-course gourmet menu for residents, eg, seafood tortellini; loin of veal with smoky creamed lentils. 'The mouth-watering puddings' have been especially enjoyed, also 'the gorgeous array of home-baked breads'. Guests rotate to different tables each night, so that all get a turn for the best views. As for the 'large, warm, sunlit' bedrooms: 'Ours was delightful, with luxurious bathroom and tempting exotica in the fruit bowl.'

Open 1 Feb–3 Nov. Lunch not served. **Rooms** 10 double. **Facilities** 2 lounges, bar, 2 dining rooms, conservatory. 12-hectare grounds. **Location** 40 miles from Knock airport. 9 miles NW of Boyle, off N4 Dublin–Sligo. Turn E at Castlebaldwin. **Credit cards** All major cards accepted. **Terms** B&B €120–€233. Set dinner €55.

COOPERSHILL   relaxed

Riverstown
Co. Sligo

Tel 00 353 71-65108
Fax 00 353 71-65466
Email ohara@coopershill.com
Website www.coopershill.com

Brian and Lindy O'Hara's 'absolutely perfect' country hotel in 'a glorious Palladian mansion' is much liked. 'Excellent housekeeping, crisp decor, large very comfortable bed, great attention to detail,' say visitors. 'The house is welcoming, run in a relaxed style by charming hosts.' Other praise: 'A lovely place with a nice house-party feeling.' Set in a large estate, with the river Arrow flowing through, it is near the knobbly hills that Yeats loved (his grave is nearby). The O'Haras (she is the chef) have a 'wonderful staff'; a parrot and friendly dogs help with the 'comfortable, lived-in feel'; antiques are real. Dinner, by candlelight, with family silver and glass, starts at 8.30 or so and can be leisurely – all guests are served each course at the same time – but diners talk to each other. The five-course meal is usually thought 'superlatively good'. Breakfasts include fresh fruit juices, 'superior porridge'. The bedrooms are 'large, and luxuriously homely'; most have a four-poster or a canopied bed.

Open 1 Apr–31 Oct. **Rooms** 8 double. No TV. **Facilities** 2 halls, drawing room, TV room, dining room; snooker room. 200-hectare estate. **Location** 11 miles SE of Sligo. Turn off N4 towards Riverstown at Drumfin; follow *Coopershill* signs. **Credit cards** All major cards accepted. **Terms** B&B €85–€128. Set dinner €42–€48.

ENNISCOE HOUSE   heritage

Castlehill, nr Ballina
Co. Mayo

Tel 00 353 96-31112
Fax 00 353 96-31773
Email mail@enniscoe.com
Website www.enniscoe.com

'Nice house, nice owner, excellent food and wine,' says a visitor returning to Susan Kellett's handsome Georgian country house, long enjoyed by guests. It stands quietly in large grounds beside Lough Conn, west of Ballina. Mrs Kellett's family have lived here for centuries, and now she runs it as a private hotel. She also operates an active heritage centre, helping today's many returning emigrants to trace their Irish roots. 'Our superior room was enormous. The simple five-course dinners are typical Irish country house fare, very appetising, served by two pleasant girls. Breakfast was good. But this old house was sometimes a bit cold in winter.' 'We enjoyed sitting in front of the peat fire after a long walk, with a drink.' The house contains elegant 18th-century plasterwork, a sweeping staircase, and two large sitting rooms with their original furniture, family portraits and bookcases; family memorabilia are everywhere, and polished wood floors with rugs. Some bedrooms have a comfortable four-poster; three overlook the lough.

Open 1 Apr–31 Oct. Dining room closed midday. **Rooms** 2 suites, 4 double. No TV. **Facilities** 2 sitting rooms, dining room. **Location** 40 miles from Knock airport. Take N5 from Charlestown to Castlebar. *Enniscoe House* is 2 miles S of Crossmolina on R315 to Pontoon. **Credit cards** Amex, MasterCard, Visa. **Terms** B&B: single €90–€105, double €152–€176. Set dinner €40.

SHANNON
(FlyBE, Ryanair)

The airport is 15 miles north-west of Limerick.

MOY HOUSE   **welcoming**

Lahinch   *Tel* 00 353 65-708 2800
Co. Clare   *Fax* 00 353 65-708 2500
              Email moyhouse@eircom.net
              Website www.moyhouse.com

'Set on a headland, in rugged dramatic landscape, with stunning views over Lahinch Bay, this flat white building, topped by a tower, has a Gothic feel outside,' writes a visitor. 'But inside it is warm and welcoming, efficiently and sensitively managed by Bernadette Merry'. Built in the mid-18th century, it was restored with 'great style and attention to detail' in 1999. In the wide hallway are modern paintings, antique furniture, a grandfather clock. 'Our bedroom had a delightful four-poster bed, luxurious fabrics, antique furniture in rosewood and mahogany; in the bathroom were under-floor heating and a cast-iron bathtub. Breakfast came with splendid home-made muesli with strawberries, black and white puddings.' Dinner, in modern Irish style, 'good and professionally presented'.

Open All year, except Christmas/New Year. **Rooms** 6 double, 3 single. **Facilities** Ramp. Drawing room with honesty bar, dining room. **Location** 30 miles NW of Shannon. 1 mile S of Lahinch, on Milltown Malbay coast road. **Credit cards** Amex, MasterCard, Visa. **Terms** B&B: single €127–€155, double €200–€229. Set dinner €45.

GREGANS CASTLE   luxury

Ballyvaughan   *Tel* 00 353 65-707 7005
Co. Clare   *Fax* 00 353 65-707 7111
                                 Email res@gregans.ie
                                 Website www.gregans.ie

'A lovely, luxurious place to stay,' says an inspector of this country house hotel, set on a hill above Galway Bay, on the edge of the Burren. It has been owned for 30 years by Moira and Peter Haden and is managed by their son Simon. 'The hall and drawing room are elegantly furnished, with interesting artefacts, paintings and photographs. Our bedroom outlook was superb, across the Burren's magical rock scenery. Comfort was total: good mahogany furniture, bathroom well fitted, but water not hot on our arrival. Dinner was fair (confit of duck; pan-fried beef, etc). Breakfast was good.' Its buffet includes local organic produce, such as home-made bread. The dining room has views of the sun setting over Galway Bay. Downstairs, turf fires and paintings of local characters 'create an Irish feel'. There is live classical harp or piano music during dinner, and Irish folk and jazz in the *Corkscrew Bar*, popular for pre-dinner drinks.

Open 12 Mar–late Oct. **Rooms** 6 suites, 16 double. No TV. **Facilities** Hall, lounge/library, bar, dining room. 5-hectare grounds. **Location** N18 to Ennis; NW on N85 to Lahinch; on N67 to Ennistymon; N67 to Ballyvaughan. Hotel at foot of Corkscrew Hill, 3½ miles SW of Ballyvaughan. **Credit cards** Amex, MasterCard, Visa. **Terms** B&B: single €110–€270, double €160–€290, suite €270–€440. Set lunch €25, dinner €49.50.

ITALY

ALGHERO/CAGLIARI
(Ryanair, Volareweb)

Ryanair flies to Alghero on the north-west coast of Sardinia; Volareweb flies to Cagliari in the south-east.

CAMISADU — **farmstay**

Casella postale 22	*Tel* 00 39 0368 3479502
Località Camisadu	*Website* www.sardinia.net/agritur
Oliena	
08025 Nuoro, Sardinia	

A simple *Agriturismo* (farmstay) offering a taste of rural life in the centre-east of this beautiful island. 'It would not suit the fastidious,' says a visitor, who found it 'fairly basic, but extremely enjoyable'. It looks over a broad valley to Orgosolo on the horizon. There is a new dining room where guests share tables, each with a blue-and-white checked cloth, and enjoy 'wonderful farm food: salami and ham; ravioli stuffed with potato and cheese; wild boar; pecorino'. 'Our bedroom was compact and unheated. You sit in the warm dining room by an open fire of olive wood.' There is a shared, 'but spotless', bathroom. 'The welcome from the Fele family was warm, and the cost was embarrassingly low.'

Open All year. **Rooms** 3 double, 1 triple. No en suite facilities. **Facilities** TV room, reading room, dining room. 8-hectare farm. **Location** 2 km SW of Oliena, on Orgosolo road. Parking. **Credit cards** None accepted. **Terms** D,B&B €47–€52.

SU GOLOGONE   panoramic

Località Su Gologone
Oliena
08025 Nuoro, Sardinia

Tel 00 39 0784 287512
Fax 00 39 0784 287668
Email gologone@tin.it
Website www.sugologone.it

'Like a small village', the Palimodde family's 'highly original' hotel is near a small town in the 'wild and hilly' centre-east of the island. 'The position is breathtaking': it is on the lower slopes of the Supramonte massif. Bedrooms are in houses and cottages dotted among 'well-groomed' gardens, arcades and alleys (lots of steps). They have white walls, blue doors, pink-tiled roofs, courtyards with cacti; some have a balcony facing the mountains. Inside are terracotta floors, local furniture and fabrics. 'Ours was large, well furnished.' Large paintings and sculptures adorn the arched lobby; local handicrafts (woven baskets, etc) line the corridors. Quiet patios have seats with bright cushions. Carcasses of sheep, wild boar and sucking pigs turn on the spit over the log fire in the juniper-beamed *ristorante tipico*, to be served with rustic breads, local wines, traditional desserts of honey, pastry and almonds. Breakfasts include fresh fruit salads and pastries. There's a swimming pool, 'big enough for proper swimming'. 'Service levels were generally high,' said our inspectors.

Open 20 Dec–6 Jan, 20 Mar–5 Nov. **Rooms** 8 suites, 60 double. **Facilities** Reading room, bar, 3 dining rooms. Garden: dining terrace; heated swimming pool. **Location** 6 km NE of Oliena. Parking. **Credit cards** All major cards accepted. **Terms** B&B: single €105–€151, double €135–€200, suite €195–€284; D,B&B €112–€170 per person.

ANCONA
(Ryanair)

The airport is 10 km west of the town.

HOTEL EDEN GIGLI   child-friendly

Viale Morelli 11   *Tel* 00 39 071 9330652
Numana   *Fax* 00 39 071 9330930
60026 Ancona   *Email* info@giglihotels.com
                                    Website www.giglihotels.com

The Gigli family's cheerful white holiday hotel, 'smart but
informal', and good for a family holiday, sits on white cliffs
looking over trees to the sea and a private beach (a short,
steep walk up, but free transport by jeep is offered). It is 20
kilometres south-east of Ancona. 'We loved it,' said
enthusiastic reporters. 'Our children liked the playground,
and the pool. Our third-floor room was large enough for the
four of us to sleep soundly.' 'Service is smooth and
unobtrusive, the people are friendly, the setting is beautiful.'
In the large, marble-floored dining room, dinner includes an
antipasto buffet, home-made pasta, lots of seafood.
Vegetables, eggs and wine come from the family's farm.

Open Apr–Oct. **Rooms** 3 suites, 29 double, 4 single. **Facilities**
TV room, bar, restaurant; terrace. Park; garden: 3 sea-water
swimming pools, whirlpool, tennis, children's playground, 'zoo'.
Location Near church: edge of village. **Restrictions** No babies
July/Aug. **Credit cards** Amex, MasterCard, Visa. **Terms** B&B:
single €75, double €95, suite €150; D,B&B €85–€115 per person.
Full alc €40.

HOTEL EMILIA   smart

Collina di Portonovo 149
Portonovo
60020 Ancona

Tel 00 39 071 801145
Fax 00 39 071 801330
Email info@hotelemilia.com
Website www.hotelemilia.com

In the Cònero Park, in a protected area of great natural beauty near Ancona in the Marche, this beautiful white building was constructed in 1964 by Elia Dubbini and Lamberto Fiorini to house their notable collection of contemporary art. Now a smart hotel, it stands alone on a natural terrace above the sea, amid broom, oaks and lavender fields. In front, a sheer gorse-topped cliff towers above a wonderful white sandy bay: 'stunning views of sea and coast'. This is a family affair: Maurizio, son of the founders, runs it with aunt Elsa, sister Raffaella and other relatives. There is an Olympic-size swimming pool in the garden, and summer meals, 'based on grandma Emilia's traditional recipes of the region', are served alfresco or in the spacious restaurant. Wine comes from the family's vineyard. A shuttle takes guests down to the rocky beach. Six electric bicycles are available for guests' use. Jazz concerts are sometimes held.

Open 22 Feb–22 Dec. Restaurant closed Mon. **Rooms** 3 suites, 26 double, 2 single. **Facilities** Lift. Lounge, TV room, bar, restaurant. Garden: swimming pool, bar/gazebo. **Location** 12 km SE of Ancona. Parking. **Credit cards** All major cards accepted. **Terms** B&B: single €105–€180, double €150–€240, suite €260–€400; D,B&B (min. 3 days; obligatory 1 week Aug) €135–€220 per person.

LOCANDA DELLA VALLE NUOVA   eco-friendly

La Cappella 14   *Tel/Fax* 00 39 0722 330303
Sagrata di Fermignano   *Email* info@vallenuova.it
61033 Pesaro e Urbino   *Website* www.vallenuova.it

'Accommodation and food of the highest standard; every detail has been thought through,' say enthusiastic visitors to this beguiling eco-friendly set-up. Near Urbino, with its magnificent ducal palace, it is surrounded by a landscape of gentle rolling hills that 'radiates beauty and tranquillity'. The architect owner, Augusto Savini, who believes that 'one should tread lightly on the earth', runs it with his wife and daughter, Adriana and Giulia, as a smoke-free, piped music-free, little guest house. 'Service is highly personal.' The simple, attractive bedrooms are well insulated, the house is solar heated, and in the open-style sitting room/library there is a 'cosy log fire'. Mother and daughter cook and serve the set five-course dinner, using seasonal ingredients, many grown on the family's surrounding organic farm: 'The *pièce de résistance* is rose jam, tasting of the fragrance of the flowers.' The large swimming pool in the garden is 'lovingly cared for' by Mr Savini. 'He brought us figs from his trees as we watched our daughter swim.'

Open 25 June–7 Nov. Dining room closed midday. **Rooms** 6 double. **Facilities** Lounge/library, dining room. Garden. **Location** 12 km S of Urbino, 3.5 km from Fermignano. Awkward to find: consult website. Parking. **Restrictions** No smoking. No children under 12. **Credit cards** None accepted. **Terms** (Min. 3 nights) B&B €45; D,B&B €65. Set dinner €25. 10% supplement for single occupancy.

BARI
(Ryanair)

Bari Palese airport is 11 km west of the city.

SASSI HOTEL   heritage

Via San Giovanni Vecchio 89
Sasso Barisano
Matera 75100

Tel 00 39 0835 331009
Fax 00 39 0835 333733
Email hotelsassi@virgilio.it
Website www.hotelsassi.it

Matera is a UNESCO world heritage site, famous for its *sassi* (dwellings carved from tufa), which were inhabited until the 1960s. This 'enchanting' B&B hotel, also cut into the rock, is in the picturesque, traffic-free part of the old town ('splendidly free of signs and advertisements'), 65 km south-west of Bari. The owner, Raffaele Cristallo, 'is passionate about the restoration', say visitors. 'The bedrooms have been beautifully modernised without spoiling the old building.' Each has a terrace or balcony. Earlier guests wrote: 'Each room is unique, not at all damp or cold as you might expect. All are well equipped; ours was smallish, with modern furniture, and a view of the cathedral.' 'It was really quiet, and the buffet breakfast was fine.' No smoking throughout.

Open All year. **Rooms** 5 suites, 13 double, 4 single. **Facilities** TV room/bar, breakfast room. Terrace. **Location** Centre of old town. Public parking/garage nearby. **Credit cards** All major cards accepted. **Terms** B&B: single €55, double €90, suite €130.

BOLOGNA
(easyJet, Ryanair)

easyJet flies to Bologna airport, 6 km north-west
of the city. Ryanair flies to Forlì, 60 km to the east.

HOTEL DEI COMMERCIANTI   high-class

Via de' Pignattari   *Tel* 00 39 051 233052
40124 Bologna   *Fax* 00 39 051 224733

Email commercianti@inbo.it
Website www.bolognahotel.net

This 'high-class hotel, just off the main square', is owned by
the Orsi family, who also own the *Orologio* (see next entry).
'Remarkably silent for its position', it has 'friendly, helpful
staff', says a visitor, 'and there are nice touches such as
bicycles for guests' use – great for cycle-friendly Bologna –
and Internet access. From our lovely beamed suite under the
eaves, we could practically look into the cathedral. Bologna
is unjustifiably neglected on the tourist trail. It is lovely, and
the food is great – don't miss eating in the wonderful
Drogheria della Rosa.'

Open All year. **Rooms** 5 suites, 22 double, 7 single. **Facilities**
Lift. Hall, lounge; Internet point, breakfast room. **Location** Centre
of old town, near Piazza Maggiore. Garage (€26 a night). **Credit
cards** All major cards accepted. **Terms** B&B: single €169–€220,
double €235–€311, suite €340–€454.

HOTEL OROLOGIO   central

Via IV Novembre 10   *Tel* 00 39 051 231253
40123 Bologna   *Fax* 00 39 051 260552
                                Email hotoro@tin.it
                        Website www.bolognahotel.net

'Superbly located' if 'not easy to find by car', this 'well-managed hotel' stands by the main square, facing the clock (*orologio*) on the civic tower. It has views of old houses and monuments, and is well placed for city-centre shopping. 'The reception staff are most helpful,' says a visitor. 'Much thought has been given to making guests comfortable.' 'Lovely bedrooms', some with a balcony, are distributed over five floors (but 'the small lift does not serve the ground floor; it begins after a flight and a half of stairs'). One guest disliked the fluorescent lights in his bedroom, which 'gave off a ghastly light'. Newspapers are available in the first-floor lounge, and in the adjacent breakfast room there is a 'remarkably varied buffet', sometimes marred by 'loud conversations carried on, almost on top of one, by the staff'. Plenty of good restaurants nearby, eg, *Diana, Nello, Rodrigo*. The area is pedestrianised, but cars are allowed in for unloading.

Open All year. **Rooms** 1 mini-flat, 5 suites, 26 double, 2 single. **Facilities** Hall, sitting room (free Internet access), breakfast room. **Location** Near main square in pedestrianised zone. Garage, parking (expensive) nearby. **Credit cards** All major cards accepted. **Terms** B&B: single €125–€220, double €180–€311, suite €280–€454.

LOCANDA SOLAROLA   gourmet

Via Santa Croce 5   *Tel* 00 39 0542 670102
Castel Guelfo di Bologna   *Fax* 00 39 0542 670222
40023 Bologna   *Email* solarola@imola.queen.it
                                     Website www.locandasolarola.com

In 1985, Antonella, a publicist in Bologna, met Valentino
Scardovi, an architect with a passion for fine food. Leaving
city life for the quiet countryside, they rebuilt two old
houses next to a villa, and created a luxurious restaurant-
with-rooms. They promise 'the atmosphere of a very English
private residence, priceless bric-a-brac, ancient carpets, lace
curtains, linen sheets and great-grandmother's unique
recipes'. A recent comment: 'The cooking (by Antonella)
was consistently delicious; its subtleties fully justified the
Michelin star.' The long wine list 'has some excellent local
Sangiovese and Ronco varieties'. In summer, you dine in a
gazebo, surrounded by flowers. 'There is a lot of interior
decoration, charming and often idiosyncratic.' Bedrooms, all
different, are named after flowers: 'Ours, big, quiet,
comfortable, had a splendid bed and shower. Breakfast was
modest but good.' The staff are friendly and 'exceptionally
helpful'.

Open All year. Restaurant closed 3 weeks Jan. **Rooms** I suite, 13
double. **Facilities** Lounge, bar, restaurant. Garden; swimming
pool. **Location** 28 km E of Bologna. From A14, exit Castel San
Pietro Terme: right towards Medicina; after 4.9 km, right to Via San
Paolo, right to Via Santa Croce. Follow *locanda*'s signs I km.
Credit cards All major cards accepted. **Terms** B&B: single
€130–€150, double €180–€210, suite €215–€336; D,B&B €50
added per person.

GENOA
(Ryanair)

The airport is 6 km from the city centre. Our recommendations are along the Ligurian Riviera.

HOTEL BEAU RIVAGE   **seafront**

Lungomare Roma 82	*Tel/Fax* 00 39 0182 640585
Alassio	*Email* b.rivage@libero.it
17021 Savona	*Website* www.hotelbeaurivage.it

With its long beach of fine sand, Alassio is a popular resort on the Ligurian Riviera, some 80 km west of Genoa. At the far end of the seafront stands this elegant arcaded 18th-century building, run by its friendly owners, Adèle and Juanito Salada. Unpretentious ('quite attractive', say recent guests), it has 'pleasant sitting areas', arched and frescoed ceilings, and a 'remarkable collection of art books and journals'. The buffet breakfast is served in a 'bright and pleasant' room. The simple half-board dinner has three choices each for first and main course: typical Ligurian dishes. Bedrooms are 'small but adequate, reasonably lit'.

Open 26 Dec–17 Oct. **Rooms** 3 suites (50 m), 17 double, 3 single. **Facilities** 2 lounges, restaurant. Garden. **Location** 800 m W of centre. Parking for guests nearby. **Credit cards** All major cards accepted. **Terms** B&B: single €53–€93, double €106–€140; D,B&B (min. 3 days) €57–€95 per person.

HOTEL CENOBIO DEI DOGI   easy-going

Via N Cuneo 34
Camogli
16032 Genova

Tel 00 39 0185 7241
Fax 00 39 0185 772796
Email reception@cenobio.it
Website www.cenobio.it

Superbly set at the southern end of this pretty fishing village, on the Ligurian coast south-east of Genoa, this large hotel is on the site of a villa once owned by the aristocratic Dogi family. A visitor returning this year for the eighth time found it 'as well run, though easy-going, as ever'. It stands above the sea in spacious grounds with pine trees and exotic plants. 'Well-managed, mildly luxurious, but cosy, it has an excellent sea-water pool, comfortable bedrooms, spacious lounges and terrace.' The view from all these is 'enchanting', and service is 'both efficient and very friendly'. 'The beach is pebbly, but bathing in the very clean sea is excellent.' The menu for the terrace near the pool has 'expanded and improved, and the restaurant meals – especially the puds – seem more interesting'. There could be noise from nearby trains, but they make travelling up and down Liguria easy. The road by the sea is car-free. Enjoyable walks in the surrounding hills.

Open All year. **Rooms** 4 suites, 88 double, 15 single. **Facilities** Lift. Lounges, restaurant; terrace; chapel. Garden: swimming pool, private beach with seasonal restaurant. **Location** Central. 15 km NW of Portofino. Parking. **Credit cards** All major cards accepted. **Terms** B&B: single €108–€151, double €150–€311, suite €258–€425; D,B&B €35 added per person.

ROMANTIK HOTEL VILLA PAGODA   historic

Via Capolungo 15
Nervi
16167 Genova

Tel 00 39 010 323200
Fax 00 39 010 321218
Email info@villapagoda.it
Website www.villapagoda.it

'A remarkable building', which claims to have been 'witness to eccentric lifestyles'. Built at the beginning of the 19th century as the home of a rich merchant, it owes its oriental style to his extensive trade with China and, it is said, his love for a Chinese girl. It stands in a small, shady park, with wide views over the Mediterranean, on the coast south of Genoa. An underground passage connects its cellar with the beach. 'Much of the furnishing, and the magnificent chandeliers in the public rooms, goes back to the Czar of Russia whose summer residence this once was. Our room, with balcony facing the sea, had many original features, and was furnished in excellent taste. Its modern bathroom had all one could wish for.' Period furniture abounds; floors are of antique Carrara marble. 'Dinner, excellently prepared, included pasta alla Genovese (pesto is a local speciality).' There are 'luscious' gardens, where summer meals are served under white parasols, and a gate with access to 'the (mostly uninteresting) beach'.

Open All year. **Rooms** 3 triple, 3 suites, 11 double. **Facilities** Lift. Lounge, piano bar, restaurant. **Location** Central. 11 km SE of Genoa. Parking. **Credit cards** All major cards accepted. **Terms** Room: single €112–€195, double €144–€280, suite €360–€770. Breakfast €13. D,B&B €48 added per person.

MILAN
(bmibaby, easyJet, Ryanair)

EasyJet flies to Linate, 12 km east of the city.
Bmibaby and Ryanair fly to Bergamo,
50 km north-east of Milan, close to lakes
Como and Iseo.

HOTEL MANZONI   city value

Via Santo Spirito 20   *Tel* 00 39 02 76005700
20121 Milan   *Fax* 00 39 02 784212
                                         Email hotel.manzoni@tin.it
                                         Website www.hotelmanzoni.com

'The location is excellent, especially once you get the hang of the tram system,' says a visitor to this unpretentious B&B hotel. It is in 'an old alley lined with *palazzi*'. Nearby are chic shopping streets; the *duomo* and La Scala are ten minutes' walk away. 'Our spacious, comfortable room had a particularly good bathroom. Staff were welcoming. The buffet breakfast was lovely: hot items, including scrambled eggs, were cooked to order.' Furnishings are 'simple and tasteful'; rates 'very reasonable'. Some rooms might get noise from nearby houses; most are 'very quiet'. There is a small breakfast area and a bar.

Open 5 Jan–21 July, 1 Sept–23 Dec. **Rooms** 3 suites, 22 double, 27 single. **Facilities** Lift. TV room, bar, breakfast room. Courtyard. **Location** Central. Garage. **Credit cards** All major cards accepted. **Terms** Room €132–€170. Breakfast €15.

Antica Locanda dei Mercanti   discreet

Via San Tomaso 6
20121 Milan

Tel 00 39 02 8054080
Fax 00 39 02 8054090
Email locanda@locanda.it
Website www.locanda.it

Alessandro Basta now owns this discreet little B&B, but his mother, its founder, Paola Ora, writes that she is still 'continuously present'. She adds: 'No noisy bar; no minibar or TV in the bedrooms, but fresh flowers, a pure wool carpet, a comfortable mattress.' Just five minutes' walk from the *duomo* and La Scala, it is in a 'rather austere' office block, down winding streets in Milan's old commercial centre. No hotel sign: look for the name and buzzer on a brass panel by the large green door. A 'tiny antique' lift takes guests up from a courtyard. Some bedrooms are small, but 'lovely' rooms on the third floor, with huge windows, open on to a terrace with potted plants. Bathrooms are 'small but adequate'. The welcome is 'helpful and calm', and 'attention to detail makes you feel you are staying in a friend's guest room'. No public rooms: breakfast, 'stylishly served' in the bedroom, includes freshly squeezed orange juice and freshly baked croissants. The owners prefer payment in cash.

Open All year. **Rooms** 14 double, 2 single. **Facilities** No public rooms. **Location** Small street between Piazza Castello and Piazza Cordusio, off pedestrian zone. **Credit cards** MasterCard, Visa, 'but cash preferred'. **Terms** Room: single €119–€130, double €130–€250. Breakfast €9.

HOTEL SPADARI AL DUOMO   designer

Via Spadari 11
20123 Milan

Tel 00 39 02 72002371
Fax 00 39 02 861184
Email spadari@tin.it
Website www.spadarihotel.com

This small designer B&B hotel 'has all the good things so hard to find in big Italian city hotels', writes an enthusiast. 'Spotless, with helpful staff, great breakfast, quiet bedrooms', it is in a side street near the *duomo*, which some rooms overlook: the new room, No. 40, on the seventh floor, has the best view. The 'charming modern-romantic style' is liked: a large sculpture and fireplace by Gio Pomodoro in the hall; 'lots of blue, beechwood furniture, pleasing fabrics, extravagant flower arrangements, contemporary paintings'. 'Our pleasant room had a flower-filled balcony.' Some junior suites have a whirlpool bath. Breakfast, in the bright bar, includes fresh fruit, freshly squeezed juices, eggs, sausages, etc. It can be served, with a newspaper, in the bedroom for no extra charge. Snacks are available at the bar and from room service. 'Many good restaurants are nearby, and the staff's recommendations were spot on. A delightful base for exploring Milan.'

Open All year, except Christmas. **Rooms** 37 double, 3 single. **Facilities** Hall, winter garden, American bar/breakfast room. **Location** Central, just W of *duomo*. **Credit cards** All major cards accepted. **Terms** B&B: single €125–€228, double €175–€288.

ALBERGO BELVEDERE   elegance

Via Valassina 31   *Tel* 00 39 031 950410
Bellagio   *Fax* 00 39 031 950102
22021 Como   *Email* belveder@tin.it
                                  Website www.belvederebellagio.com

In 1880 the *Belvedere* opened as a simple *trattoria alloggio*, above a picturesque little harbour and small stony beach on Lake Como. Today, it is an elegant hotel owned by Tiziana Martinelli Manoni, a descendant of the original owners. It is liked for the 'family ambience', 'courteous staff', 'very good food and wine' and 'lovely setting'. A large white building, it stands in terraced gardens, 'full of birdsong'. Beautiful Bellagio, with its tree-shaded promenade and ancient narrow streets, is a five-minute stroll away. There are views across the lake from many bedrooms, the restaurant, the terrace where alfresco meals are served, and the swimming pool (surrounded by loungers and lawns). Some rooms look on to a side street. A recent visitor writes: 'Our bedroom, very comfortable, with large bathroom and dressing room, in a newly restored building, opened on to lawn and garden. In the lovely dining room, the friendly waitress really knew her wines.' Traditional dishes include fish from the lake. 'Excellent breakfasts.'

Open 1 Apr–31 Oct. **Rooms** 2 suites, 62 double, 4 single. **Facilities** Lift. Lounge, reading room, TV room, breakfast room, bar, restaurant. Garden: terrace restaurant. **Location** 300 m from centre of Bellagio (55 km from Bergamo). Parking. **Credit cards** All major cards accepted. **Terms** B&B: single €95–€110, double €135–€238, suite €280–€342; D,B&B: single €120–€137, double €185–€292, suite €330–€396.

RELAIS I DUE ROCCOLI   panoramic

Via S. Bonomelli
Iseo
25049 Brescia

Tel 00 39 030 9822977
Fax 00 39 030 9822980
Email relais@idueroccoli.com
Website www.idueroccoli.com

In an immaculate garden, surrounded by woods and steep slopes, Guido Anessi's 17th-century former hunting lodge (Relais du Silence) stands high above Lake Iseo (one of Italy's smallest lakes). 'It has everything,' says a devotee. 'Lovely location, pleasing building and furnishings, excellent food; above all, superb staff. One of the best hotels we know.' Panoramic views over the lake are 'truly magnificent': it can be seen from some bedrooms. Another visitor's room 'combined rusticity and elegance: beautiful wood-beamed ceiling, painted shutters, iron bed'. Some bedroom walls may be thin. The restaurant looks over the gardens: its stone terrace is adorned with pots of roses and geraniums. 'The dinners were delicious, with courteous service': cuisine is traditional, using lake fish, home-made ham and salami, organic home-grown fruit and vegetables. 'Breakfasts were excellent, with a juicer that squeezed whole oranges.' Vincenzo Agoni, the manager, 'does not encourage package tours'. Around are the Franciacorta vineyards, which produce Italy's best sparkling wines.

Open 15 Mar–30 Oct. **Rooms** 3 suites, 15 double (1 in cottage), 1 single. **Facilities** Lift. Lounge, bar, restaurant with terrace. Park: garden, unheated swimming pool. **Location** 5 km E of Iseo, on road to Polaveno. **Credit cards** All major cards accepted. **Terms** Room: single €93, double €124–€140, suite €165. Breakfast €9.50. D,B&B €95–€125 per person.

GRAND HOTEL VICTORIA   *grandeur*

Via Benedetto Castelli 7
Menaggio
22017 Como

Tel 00 39 0344 32003
Fax 00 39 0344 32992
Email hotelvictoria@palacehotel.it
Website www.palacehotel.it

Wide staircases, Liberty-style chandeliers, and rooms
decorated with stucco works and gold, show the *belle époque*
origins of this 'true Grand Hotel'. Fairly recently renovated, it
stands in mature gardens looking across Lake Como. The
views over the lake from the front of the house are a 'real
plus point', says a visitor. 'Occasional evening traffic made it
sensible to keep the windows closed (excellent
soundproofing), and one night, we slept peacefully through
the departure of a bride and groom from their wedding
party.' Others have said: 'The highly professional staff were
wonderfully friendly. Our bedroom, though nothing special,
was quiet and had a stunning lake view.' Some rooms have a
balcony. One visitor found the beds 'not very comfortable'. In
summer, meals are taken on the covered terrace overlooking
the lake: 'An excellent four-course dinner.' Breakfast is a
generous buffet. Picturesque Menaggio has a beautiful long
promenade, a pretty harbour and lakeside piazza; also
'proper shops' and it 'doesn't feel touristy'.

Open All year. Restaurant closed midday winter/public holidays.
Rooms 2 suites, 42 double, 11 single. **Facilities** Lifts. Salon, bar,
restaurant, veranda restaurant. Garden: terrace, swimming pool;
lake frontage. **Location** 32 km N of Como. N end of village, by
lake. **Credit cards** All major cards accepted. **Terms** B&B: single
€75–€116, double €179–€215, suite €312–€420; D,B&B €32 added
per person.

NAPLES
(easyJet, Thomsonfly)

The airport is 7 km west of the city.

HOTEL MIRAMARE   seafront

Via Nazario Sauro 24   *Tel* 00 39 081 7647589
80132 Naples   *Fax* 00 39 081 7640775
                          Email info@hotelmiramare.com
                          Website www.hotelmiramare.com

An 'extremely pleasant' small B&B hotel on the seafront, across the 'quite busy' road along the Bay of Naples. From the 'lovely rooftop terrace' where the 'fine buffet breakfast' is served, it has wonderful views of Vesuvius and the bay. Built in 1914 as an aristocratic villa, it has Liberty-style decor, and it is just ten minutes' walk from the central Via Chiaia area. 'The place is enlivened by the warmth and efficiency of the manager, Enzo Rosolino, and his staff,' say visitors. 'Traffic noise very slight.' 'Our room had two balconies, and fine-quality linen sheets and feather pillows.' Under the same ownership are two nearby eating places: *La Cantinella* (the city's only *Michelin*-starred restaurant) and *Il Posto Accanto*.

Open All year. **Rooms** 30. **Facilities** Lift. Breakfast room. Terrace. **Location** 10 mins' walk from centre. **Credit cards** All major cards accepted. **Terms** B&B (min. 2 nights weekends): single €134–€184, double €151–€290.

GRAND HOTEL PARKER'S   doyenne

Corso Vittorio Emanuele 135   *Tel* 00 39 081 7612474
80121 Naples   *Fax* 00 39 081 663527
                                      Email info@grandhotelparkers.it
                                      Website www.grandhotelparkers.com

This is the 'doyenne of good Neapolitan hotels'. 'Not tremendously central, it makes a good base for visiting this fascinating city': it stands on the slopes of the Vomero hill. Named after George Parker Bidder, who bought it after staying here in 1889 (he lived in what is now the 'presidential suite'), it offers 'old-fashioned comfort, rather than modern luxury; good food and friendly service', according to guests. Front bedrooms have 'stunning views' over the city to Capri, the Amalfi peninsula and Vesuvius. So does the rooftop restaurant, *George's*, which has a terrace for outside dining. 'Our room was delightful, decorated with understated elegance (antique furniture). We liked the charming notes, left on the pillows at night, informing us of the weather next day.' Original paintings and sculptures fill the building, and the library has a large collection of 19th-century books. Clark Gable, Bernard Shaw, Lenin and Oscar Wilde have all stayed here. A health centre (with massage, Turkish bath and beauty treatments) is new.

Open All year. **Rooms** 10 suites, 65 double, 8 single. **Facilities** Lounges, library, piano bar, restaurant with terrace; health centre. **Location** Vomero hill, above Porto di Mergellina. Garage. **Credit cards** All major cards accepted. **Terms** B&B: single €235–€245, double €295–€330, suite €515–€1,025. Full alc €50.

ALBERGO SANSEVERO   value

Via S.M. Costantinopoli 101   *Tel* 00 39 081 7901000
80138 Naples   *Fax* 00 39 081 211698
                                     Email albergo.sansevero@libero.it
                                     Website www.albergosansevero.it

In the *centro storico*, this 'wonderful, if somewhat dilapidated' old *palazzo* offers accommodation that is 'both classy and cheap'. It has 'high ceilings, large rooms, serviceable bathrooms, inexpensive modern furniture, obliging staff'. No hotel sign: arriving guests are confronted by 'magnificently closed doors'. Some rooms have a balcony overlooking Via Costantinopoli and 'the city's number-one meeting spot, Piazza Bellini' – they can be noisy. The simple breakfast is served in the room or in the next-door café: one recent visitor thought it 'inadequate even by Italian standards'. Under the same ownership are the *Soggiorno Sansevero*, close by, on the first floor of the Palazzo Sansevero ('safe, atmospheric, reasonably priced; bedroom as big as a ballroom'), the *Sansevero Degas* (in a building once owned by the painter's family), and the *Palazzo Doria d'Angri*. The latter, which has nine bedrooms, offers an evening meal for €15, and has some large, splendidly frescoed rooms for functions, concerts, etc. Also recommended for meals: the *Trattoria da Carmine,* Via dei Tribunali.

Open All year. **Rooms** 35 double. 29 with facilities en suite. **Facilities** Lounge (bar/meal service), 3 TV rooms. **Location** Historic centre. **Credit cards** All major cards accepted. **Terms** B&B: single €75–€88, double €95–€130. Evening meal €15.

PALERMO
(Ryanair)

Palermo airport is on the north-west tip of Sicily.

MASSIMO PLAZA HOTEL   **palazzo**

Via Maqueda 437
Palermo
90133 Sicily

Tel 00 39 091 325657
Fax 00 39 091 325711
Email booking@massimoplazahotel.com
Website www.massimoplazahotel.com

With 'a stylish manner at a moderate price', Nicola Farruggio's B&B is in part of an old *palazzo* in the *centro storico* of this fascinating city. Opposite are Piazza Verdi and the ornate Teatro Massimo, Europe's third largest opera house. Bedrooms are 'simple, but comfortable'. Some have a balcony overlooking the plaza; quieter ones are on the side. 'All have effective double glazing.' The 'basic' breakfast is usually brought to the bedroom, but it can be taken in the bar/lounge, with potted plants, where tea and drinks are served. 'Staff were friendly, particularly reception, and the porter who parked our car,' said inspectors. Good restaurants, eg, *Santandrea*, are nearby.

Open All year. **Rooms** 1 suite, 14 double. **Facilities** Bar/lounge/TV room. **Location** Central, opposite Teatro Massimo. Parking. Airport shuttle. **Credit cards** All major cards accepted. **Terms** B&B: single €105–€130, double €160–€185.

HOTEL ELIMO   value

Via Vittorio Emanuele 75	*Tel* 00 39 0923 869377
Erice	*Fax* 00 39 0923 869252
91016 Sicily	*Email* hotelelimo@siciliaindettaglio.it
	Website www.charmerelax.com

'Not cheap, but probably the best value of our tour,' says a visitor who found 'a warm welcome and excellent family-based service' at the Tilotta family's hotel. In the *centro storico* of this ancient mountain village in the north-west of Sicily, this restored building has 'magnificent' views of Trápani below. 'Our excellent double room, newly furnished, had a sitting area and a comfortable, large bed. The superb dinner was enlivened by an invitation to the kitchen where the chef/proprietor, Carmelo Tilotta, an Albert Einstein lookalike, showed us how to cook tuna on a volcanic stove. Breakfast was above average.' There is a panoramic terrace for summer meals. The hotel, a 'clever blend of new (bedrooms) and old (public areas, with pictures and books)', is in a narrow street best not negotiated by car: you should park in the public car park and walk up (100 metres); luggage will be fetched.

Open All year. Restaurant closed January. **Rooms** 3 suites, 17 double, 1 single. **Facilities** Lift. Lounge, bar, restaurant. Terrace, small garden. **Location** Central. 96 km W of Palermo. **Credit cards** All major cards accepted. **Terms** B&B: single €75–€129, double €110–€196; D,B&B: single €85–€140, double €210–€250.

AL POGGETTO   rural

Contrada Pianetto   *Tel* 00 39 091 8570213
Santa Cristina Gela   *Fax* 00 39 091 6704936
90030 Sicily   *Email* info@alpoggetto.it
                            Website www.alpoggetto.it

An hour's drive south from Palermo up 'beautiful mountain roads' is this *Azienda Agricola*, 700 metres above sea level and surrounded by olive and cherry trees. A visitor found it 'relaxed' and 'run with some style' by the owners Lucrezia Panvini and her 'voluble' husband. She is 'always on hand to make sure your glass is never empty'; he is 'happy to advise guests on travel'. The 'lovely' bedrooms have local antique furniture; front rooms look over the pretty pool and garden. The *à la carte* restaurant, serving Sicilian dishes, was thought 'unimaginative'. Meals are taken outside in fine weather. Animals include the owners' 'gaggle of friendly dogs', horses on the Arab stud farm, and a pet donkey which 'casually wanders by to look at the guests'.

Open All year. **Rooms** 4 suites, 7 double. **Facilities** Lift. Lounge, reading room, bar, restaurant. Large garden: swimming pool, sauna. **Location** 40 km S of Palermo airport, 22 km S of Palermo. Through Altofonte, then up hill of Santa Cristina Gela. Parking. **Credit cards** Some accepted (check with hotel). **Terms** B&B: double €90–€100, suite €120–€130.

PISA
(Ryanair, Thomsonfly)

Pisa airport, 2 km south of the city,
serves the main Tuscan towns and cities.

HOTEL LA LUNA   value

Via Fillungo, Corte Compagni 12   *Tel* 00 39 0583 493634
55100 Lucca   *Fax* 00 39 0583 490021
                                       Email laluna@onenet.it
                                       Website www.hotellaluna.com

Visitors to Nino Barbieri's modest B&B hotel, in a shopping
street near the remarkable Piazza Anfiteatro of this lovely
walled Renaissance city (22 kilometres north-east of Pisa),
found the management 'most helpful', and their room 'very
pleasant'. Public rooms are plain and modern; one has a
frescoed ceiling, so do some bedrooms. Most bedrooms are
small, 'but nicely done: exposed beams, a good shower' (no
baths). 'Quiet, apart from a local bar's music; we heard birds
in the morning.' The buffet breakfast is 'modest but
generous', or you can take a coffee and croissant in the bar.
The city is largely pedestrianised, but you can drive to the
hotel's garage (200 m).

Open 7 Feb–7 Jan. **Rooms** 2 suites, 21 double, 7 single. **Facilities**
Lift. TV/meeting room, bar, breakfast room. **Location** Approach
from Piazza S. Maria inside city walls. **Credit cards** All major cards
accepted. **Terms** Room €90–€160. Breakfast €10.50.

LOCANDA AL COLLE   hillside retreat

Fraz. S Lucia 103   *Tel* 00 39 0584 915195
Camaiore   *Fax* 00 39 0584 917053
55041 Lucca   *Email* locandaalcolle@interfree.it
                           Website www.locandaalcolle.it

Near the coast, in Tuscany's northernmost province, this creeper-covered, small stone guest house stands isolated in an olive grove on a hillside. The seaside resorts of Marina di Pietrasanta and Viareggio (fine sandy beaches) are not far away, but here, in the hills, 'the air is cooler'. There is a lounge, but the main sitting and dining area is the large veranda with views through olive trees towards the coast. The decor is 'charming, quite plain'; bedrooms are 'of a high standard'. 'Delicious, self-service breakfasts' include home-made muesli, fresh-baked croissants. The multilingual owner, Mario Lucchesi, and manager, Riccardo Barsottelli, say they can offer a 'professional massage'. They sometimes provide an evening meal; otherwise *Il Vignaccio*, in the nearby hill village of Santa Lucia, is recommended: 'Splendid views, good food.' Lucca, Pisa and Florence are within easy touring distance. Close by are the marble quarries of Carrara.

Open All year except winter (check with hotel). **Rooms** 1 self-contained studio, 5 double. **Facilities** Lounge, small sitting area; veranda. **Location** 18 km NW of Lucca, 4 km E of Pietrasanta. From A11/A12: exit Viareggio Nord, follow signs to Camaiore. At 3rd traffic light, left to Via Dietro Monte; up hill to B&B sign. **Credit cards** None accepted. **Terms** B&B: single €70–€100, double €90–€125, studio €500–€750.

LOGGIATO DEI SERVITI   favourite

Piazza SS. Annunziata 3   *Tel* 00 39 055 289592
50122 Florence   *Fax* 00 39 055 289595
Email info@loggiatodeiservitihotel.it
Website www.loggiatodeiservitihotel.it

'Utterly charming', with 'excellent service' and 'tastefully designed rooms', the Gattai family's much-loved B&B is in 'one of Florence's loveliest squares'. Built in 1527 for the order of the Serviti Fathers, it is 'rich in atmosphere, tranquillity and comfort', though one guest has said: 'The breakfasts have improved with time; the lift has not.' 'Gracefully restored, in understated style', the stone-vaulted building has polished oak floors, iron or wooden bedsteads, efficient air-conditioning. Bedrooms vary in size and quality; those at the rear have been found 'utterly quiet', though some may 'lack character'. 'Ours was large and bright.' 'Ours had views of the floodlit *duomo*, and a handsomely canopied bed.' 'Our small family suite looked over the square to gardens beyond.' Breakfasts have fresh fruit, hot croissants and rolls. On summer evenings, jazz is often played in the square, which is closed to traffic. Ten new rooms (five in an adjacent building) have recently been added.

Open All year. **Rooms** 4 suites, 28 double, 6 single. 5 in annexe. **Facilities** Lift. Lounge, reading room, bar, breakfast room. **Location** Pedestrian zone, 200 m from *duomo*. Garage service. **Credit cards** All major cards accepted. **Terms** B&B: single €90–€140, double €130–€205, suite €220–€384.

VILLA BELVEDERE   value

Via Benedetto Castelli 3   *Tel* 00 39 055 222501/2
50124 Florence   *Fax* 00 39 055 223163
                              Email reception@villa-belvedere.com
                              Website www.villa-belvedere.com

The setting of this 'friendly family hotel' is 'stunning'. It looks over Florence to the hills beyond: the *duomo* can be clearly seen, but the *autostrada* is hidden by trees. Run by two generations of the Ceschi-Perotto family ('always around'), it stands in well-kept gardens. A returning visitor found it 'as lovely as ever', adding: 'I feel happy there.' Staff are 'never obtrusive'. 'Everything is well managed.' The building may lack 'antique charm', but all is 'comfortable, spotlessly clean', and 'the facilities are excellent'. Bedrooms have a smart colour scheme, wood fittings, a spacious bathroom. 'Metal window shutters keep out city noise and early-morning sunlight.' Some rooms, good for a family, are in a little house by the small swimming pool. Breakfast is served on a veranda facing the *duomo*. 'More than adequate' snacks are available until 8.30 pm. 'You can sip a drink in the garden at night, roses scenting the air, the city lights twinkling below.' 'Very good value.' The city is a short bus ride away.

Open 1 Mar–30 Nov. **Rooms** 3 suites, 21 double, 2 single. **Facilities** Lift. 3 lounges, TV room, bar, breakfast room, snack room. **Location** E of Siena road, 2 km S of centre. Leave Florence by Porta Romana. Bus 11: stop Poggio Imperiale. **Credit cards** All major cards accepted. **Terms** B&B: single €100–€130, double €150–€207, suite €220–€260. Light alc meal €15.

ROME
(easyJet, Ryanair, Thomsonfly)

All three airlines fly to Ciampino airport,
15 km south of the city.

HOTEL BAROCCO   historic

Via della Purificazione 4 | *Tel* 00 39 06 4872001
Piazza Barberini 9 | *Fax* 00 39 06 485994
00187 Rome | *Email* info@hotelbarocco.com
 | *Website* www.hotelbarocco.com

At the foot of Via Veneto, this historic building is within easy
walking distance of the sights of ancient Rome, '*and* the
classy shopping streets'. Recently totally renovated, it has
cherry wood in the breakfast room, 'antique' stucco and
19th-century prints and oil paintings on the walls, luxurious
fabrics, and marble from Trani in the large bathrooms.
'Everything gleams with cleanliness'; the manager, Franco
Caruso, leads a 'pleasant and polite' staff. One couple 'could
not fault' their spacious suite. Others have said: 'Our room,
not large, had sturdy custom-built furniture and two large
windows overlooking a small side street. Efficient air-
conditioning and comfortable beds ensured a good night's
sleep.' The breakfast buffet is 'first rate'. No restaurant;
plenty nearby.

Open All year. **Rooms** 5 suites, 26 double, 6 single. **Facilities**
Lift, lobby, TV room, bar, breakfast room. **Location** Central:
Piazza Barberini (windows double-glazed). (Metro: Barberini)
Credit cards All major cards accepted. **Terms** B&B: single
€150–€216, double €210–€325, suite €380–€516.

HOTEL LOCARNO   Art Deco

Via della Penna 22   *Tel* 00 39 06 3610841
00186 Rome   *Fax* 00 39 06 3215249
                                  Email info@hotellocarno.com
                                  Website www.hotellocarno.com

Near the Piazza del Popolo, this Art Deco hotel opened its doors in 1925. Now extended by the acquisition of an adjacent building, it has a 'charming internal courtyard', say visitors: the ample breakfast buffet is served here or on the rooftop terrace. Many original features survive: antiques and 1950s items create a 'relaxing, undesigned' ambience. 'Our room had huge windows, efficient air-conditioning so no traffic noise. A huge chandelier hung from the high ceiling. The large bathroom had an old freestanding cast-iron bath. Housekeeping was good.' In the 'comfortable lounge area', light meals and snacks are served. 'Staff are helpful. The lovely old interiors have a slightly faded air of gentility.' Bicycles are available. The business centre has Internet facilities.

Open All year. **Rooms** 72. 6 no-smoking. **Facilities** Lift. Lounge area, bar. Courtyard. Roof garden. **Location** Central, near Piazza del Popolo. (Metro: Flaminio) **Credit cards** All major cards accepted. **Terms** B&B: single €120, double €190–€310, suite from €510.

HOTEL DEI MELLINI   luxury

Via Muzio Clementi 81
00193 Rome

Tel 00 39 06 324771
Fax 00 39 06 32477801
Email info@hotelmellini.com
Website www.hotelmellini.com

On the right bank of the Tiber, near the Vatican, this elegant hotel 'belongs to the "expensive-but-worth-it" category', says a visitor. 'The welcome is courteous, decor is modern; rooms, high-ceilinged, spacious and airy, are luxurious, as befits the price. Breakfast is sumptuous. But we could have done without the background music.' Other comments: 'The design (by an Englishman) is stylish, quite sober'; 'Our suite had a lounge with sofa and TV; in the bedroom was a further large television set, an enormous bed. Good, quiet air-conditioning.' *Bambini* are welcomed (free cribs, etc). Light meals are served in the bar, and numerous eating places are nearby.

Open All year. **Rooms** 11 suites, 2 junior suites, 63 double, 4 single. **Facilities** Lounge, breakfast room, bar. Roof terrace. **Location** Right bank of Tiber, near Vatican. Garage adjacent. **Credit cards** All major cards accepted. **Terms** B&B: single €280–€300, double €320–€350, suite €420–€840.

HOTEL PORTOGHESI   value

Via dei Portoghesi
00186 Rome

Tel 00 39 06 6864231
Fax 00 39 06 6876976
Email info@hotelportoghesiroma.com
Website www.hotelportoghesiroma.com

Within easy walking distance of the Vatican in one direction, the Forum and Coliseum in another, the Trevi Fountain and Spanish Steps in a third, this old building takes its name from the exquisite national Portuguese church nearby. It was turned into a hotel by the Sagnotti family owners more than 150 years ago. 'Excellent: clean, comfortable,' said a recent guest, 'and it won't break the bank.' Bedrooms are 'compact, but well decorated'; 'furniture is solid'. Airy corridors and landings are paved with marble. There is a roof terrace, where breakfast ('adequate, if not special') is served under lemon trees in good weather (on cooler days you sit in a glassed-in area). 'Staff are helpful.' Plenty of restaurants nearby: *La Campana* ('traditional Roman food') and *Il Bacaro* ('caters more to foreigners') have been recommended.

Open All year. **Rooms** 1 apartment (with kitchen), 4 suites, 17 double, 2 single. **Facilities** Lift. Lounge, breakfast room, roof terrace. **Location** Central, near Piazza Navona. **Credit cards** MasterCard, Visa. **Terms** B&B: single €150, double €190, suite €210–€335.

TEATRO DI POMPEO   unfussy

Largo del Pallaro 8   *Tel* 00 39 06 68300170
00186 Rome   *Fax* 00 39 06 68805531
                              Email hotel.teatrodipompeo@tiscali.it
                              Website www.hotelteatrodipompeo.it

Built on the site of Pompey's theatre (55 BC), the Cavarocchi-Mignoni family's small hotel is in the historic centre, close to Piazza Navona and the Campo de' Fiori. The four-storey terraced building is on an almost traffic-free, cobbled side street, 'ideally situated for reasonably fit walkers'. The spacious bedrooms are well kept; quietest ones (with shower) overlook the little inner courtyard. 'The staff are pleasant, service is efficient, and the breakfast coffee is good,' said one visitor. Another liked the 'unfussy decor, high dark wood ceilings, safe behind a picture (very Poirot) and functional bathroom with a powerful shower'. Breakfast is served in the old stone vault, where you can see the ancient ruins. Many reasonably priced restaurants are within walking distance.

Open All year. **Rooms** 12 double (3 in annexe, 50 m), 1 single. **Facilities** Lift. Lounge, bar with TV, breakfast room. **Location** Central, near Piazza Campo de' Fiori. **Credit cards** All major cards accepted. **Terms** B&B: single €130–€150, double €170–€190.

LA RESIDENZA   traditional

Via Emilia 22–24   *Tel* 00 39 06 4880789
00187 Rome   *Fax* 00 39 06 485721

Email hotel.la.residenza@venere.it
Website www.thegiannettihotelsgroup.com

In a 'terrific location', just off Via Veneto and not far from the Borghese Gardens, stands this old-established hotel with its yellow walls, green shutters and orange awnings. It belongs to the Giannetti group: 'Reception is run by courteous men.' Public rooms (all no-smoking, apart from the bar) have a 19th/20th-century decor. There is a weekly drinks party for residents. Free international newspapers, and video films in English and Italian, are available. The lavish breakfast buffet includes cheeses, tomatoes, fruit tarts, prosciutto, 'delicious bread'. The large front bedrooms are 'comfortable, with a big bath and decent air-conditioning', but they hear street noise and the nightclub opposite; quieter ones at the rear are smaller and darker, but some have a balcony. Housekeeping may not be perfect. No restaurant; plenty nearby.

Open All year. **Rooms** 7 suites, 17 double, 5 single. **Facilities** Lift. 2 lounges, library/bar, breakfast room; rooftop terrace. Patio. **Location** Central, off Via Veneto (rear rooms quietest). (Metro: Barberini) **Credit cards** MasterCard, Visa. **Terms** B&B: single €83–€93, double €180–€191, junior suite €207–€223.

TREVISO
(Ryanair)

Treviso airport is 30 km north-west of Venice.
Ryanair advertises it as an entry point to Venice,
but here is an alternative inland.

ALBERGO AL SOLE   bolt hole

Via Collegio 33
Asolo
31011 Treviso

Tel 00 39 0423 528111
Fax 00 39 0423 528399
Email info@albergoalsole.com
Website www.albergoalsole.com

Known as 'the city with a hundred horizons' this charming
little medieval hill town in the Veneto was once a bolt hole
for wealthy Venetians escaping the summer heat. Standing
quietly in an elevated position is Silvia De Checchi's pink and
cream 16th-century villa. She has recently opened a
panoramic restaurant, *La Terrazza*. 'Some of the junior suites
have lovely views,' says our correspondent, 'but all the
bedrooms are to be recommended. Ours was large, with
fresh fruit, lovely bedlinen, a wonderful shower. The
ambience is relaxed, but attention to detail is paramount.'
Breakfast is served on a balcony with views, or in a 'nicely
thought-out' room on a cool day.

Open All year. Restaurant may close in winter. **Rooms** 1 suite, 14
double, 8 single. **Facilities** Lift. Hall, restaurant, breakfast
room; Terrace. **Location** Central. 30 km NW of Treviso. **Credit
cards** Amex, MasterCard, Visa. **Terms** B&B: single €110–€144,
double €180–€198, suite €218–€255. Full alc €35.

TRIESTE
(Ryanair)

The airport is 34 km north-west of Trieste.
Those in the know head eastward to north-west
Croatia. Our choices are no more than
100 km from Trieste.

HOTEL VILLA ARISTON   classic

M. Tita 179	*Tel* 00 385 51 27 13 79
Opatija	*Fax* 00 385 51 27 14 94
51410 Kvarner & Highlands	*Email* office@villa-ariston.net

Within walking distance of this classic seaside resort,
popular with the aristocracy in the era of the Austro-
Hungarian Empire, is this 'very handsome villa', set on lovely
terraced gardens looking over the sea. Built in the 19th
century, renovated in 1924, it has a 'fabulous atmosphere',
say visitors. 'Our room, like most, was on the attic floor,
plain and a bit brown, but good; it had a lovely view across
the bay. The bathroom, also rather communist-retro, was
well equipped, apart from lack of plug in the wash basin.' The
'very smart' restaurant, that specialises in fish, is popular
locally, so you should reserve a table.

Open All year. **Rooms** 2 suites, 8 double. **Facilities** Lounge, bar,
dining rooms; terraces. **Location** On seafront, just outside the
town. **Credit cards** All major cards accepted. **Terms** B&B: single
€53–€73, double €82–€164, suite €178–€247.

HOTEL ANGELO D'ORO   palace

Via Svalba 38–42
Rovinj
52210 Istria

Tel 00 385 52 84 05 02
Fax 00 385 52 84 01 11
Email hotel.angelo@vip.hr
Website www.rovinj.at

In this beautiful former Venetian port, the 18th-century bishop's palace has been converted into an upmarket hotel by an Austrian architect. It is in an atmospheric narrow street in a pedestrianised area of the old town: staff will meet guests nearby, by arrangement; cars are left in reserved parking spaces. The small loggia on the top floor has a sea view. 'Our room, moderately sized and well equipped, with parquet floor, looked on to the pretty garden. We heard enthusiastic bell-ringing at 7 am from St Eufemia's church. In our modern bathroom were robes and lots of towels, but few hooks, and a faulty seal on the shower door resulted in a flooded floor. Dinner by candlelight was excellent, especially the fish, and you can choose your wine direct from the cellar, which is fun. Grappa comes on the house. Breakfast, with excellent coffee, fresh fruit, good breads and pastries, can be taken in the garden but service there tends to be slow.' The hotel has a boat for trips to the islands.

Open Mar–Sept. **Rooms** 24. **Facilities** Salons, bar, restaurant; sauna, spa bath, solarium. Garden: bar, terrace. **Location** Old town. **Credit cards** All major cards accepted. **Terms** B&B: single €67–€108, double €110–€192, suite €200–€260; D,B&B €24 added per person.

VENICE

(easyJet, Jet2, Ryanair, Thomsonfly, Volareweb)

All these airlines fly to Marco Polo airport,
a short water-bus connection from the city,
except Ryanair which flies to Treviso.

AGLI ALBORETTI   value

Accademia 884 – Dorsoduro   *Tel* 00 39 041 5230058
30123 Venice   *Fax* 00 39 041 5210158
                                   Email alborett@gpnet.it
                                   Website www.aglialboretti.com

'Colourful, pretty and understated', this unassuming little
hotel/restaurant, nicely situated near the Accademia, offers
'good value for Venice'. Owned by the Linguerri family, it is
easily reached by the water bus from the airport that goes
on to Zattere, after stopping at St Mark's Square. The rooms
are designed to give 'the homely ambience of an old
Venetian house': some have a balcony or terrace facing the
garden. 'Our good-sized bedroom, on the fourth floor, had a
simple but smart decor, solid wooden furniture, a marble
floor.' Staff are 'pleasant, if not effusive'. Meals are served in
the beamed restaurant or the ochre-walled courtyard with
its canopy of leaves and vines. 'A wonderful dinner.' The
continental breakfast is 'good'.

Open All year, except Jan/Feb, 3 weeks Aug. Restaurant closed
Wed/Thurs midday. **Rooms** 18 double, 5 single. **Facilities** Lift.
Lounge, bar, restaurant; courtyard garden. **Location** By
Accademia. **Credit cards** MasterCard, Visa. **Terms** B&B: single
€104, double €150–€180; D,B&B: €120–€149 per person.

CA' PISANI HOTEL   ultra-chic

Dorsoduro 979/a   *Tel* 00 39 041 2401411
30123 Venice   *Fax* 00 39 041 2771061
                                      Email info@capisanihotel.it
                                      Website www.capisanihotel.it

Visitors, returning for the third time, thought this 'ultra-chic' hotel, a converted 16th-century *palazzo*, 'exceptional value', particularly for Venice. Named after Vettor Pisani, the great admiral of the ancient republic, it is owned and run by the Serandrei family. The position is 'near-ideal', 'in quiet Dorsoduro, close to the Accademia' and opposite *Agli Alboretti* (see previous entry). The rooftop terrace has 'atmospheric views'. Sitting areas on most floors provide a 'peaceful refuge'. 'In many ways a design masterpiece,' another couple wrote: 'Our stunning split-level studio had possibly the most hi-tech bathroom we've seen.' Bathrooms have 'sparkling granite; terrific power shower' with 'water from six different outlets'. The decor is Italian futurist, and several guests found the banks of light switches 'seriously confusing'. 'Beds very comfortable, but air-conditioning noisy (reception will turn it off if you ask). Some rooms face the blank wall of the Accademia: it is worth asking about the view.' Staff are 'consistently friendly and helpful'. The 'refined' bar/restaurant, *La Rivista*, serves a 'limited range of meals'.

Open All year. Restaurant closed Mon. **Rooms** 29 double. **Facilities** Lift, chairlift. Lounge, restaurant/bar; roof terrace. **Location** Central, near Accademia bridge/Zattere water-bus stop. **Credit cards** All major cards accepted. **Terms** B&B: single €204–€285, double €204–€381. Full alc €35.50–€55. Min. stay 3 nights at weekends.

HOTEL CONCORDIA   17th-century casa

Calle Larga, San Marco 367   *Tel* 00 39 041 5206866
30124 Venice   *Fax* 00 39 041 5206775
                              Email venezia@hotelconcordia.it
                              Website www.hotelconcordia.it

'The only hotel in Venice with windows overlooking Piazza San Marco' – an ochre-coloured 17th-century Venetian *casa*. Recent visitors found it 'a quiet haven in a crowded area', adding: 'It could not be more central; we were very comfortable.' Others praised the 'warm, attentive staff, a pleasure to deal with, even on the Internet'. 'Our spacious double room, with tiny, flower-bedecked balcony overlooking the square, was well appointed. Water, fresh fruit and cookies awaited us. No noise from outside thanks to a well-glazed window.' Bedroom decor is in 18th-century style; Murano glass lighting fixtures; bedcovers silk damask. The breakfast buffet, in a room looking over the cathedral, 'caters for all tastes'. Snacks are available all day, and the restaurant, *La Piazzetta*, serves light lunches and candlelit dinners.

Open All year. Restaurant closed Wed night. **Rooms** 54 double, 2 single. **Facilities** Reading room, bar, restaurant. **Location** By St Mark's Square. **Credit cards** All major cards accepted. **Terms** B&B: single €130–€243, double €186–€413. Full alc €45.

HOTEL FLORA   favourite

San Marco 2283/A   *Tel* 00 39 041 5205844
30124 Venice   *Fax* 00 39 041 5228217
                                         Email info@hotelflora.it
                                         Website www.hotelflora.it

Near St Mark's Square, on a pretty street with 'some of the most expensive boutiques in Venice', Ruggero and Gioele Romanelli's B&B hotel has long been the *Good Hotel Guide*'s most popular Venetian entry. At the end of a small alley, by the Contarini Palace (Shakespeare's setting for *Othello*), 'it is quiet, even by local standards'. 'A place of great character', it has an 'old-fashioned' feel that is mostly enjoyed. A British hotelier, on his third visit, found it 'magical as ever; stuck in a time warp of genuine hospitality, undisturbed by modern management-speak'. Bedrooms vary hugely: if you book late, you get a small one (one was found cold in winter), and some bathrooms are 'cramped'. The best rooms overlook the courtyard, 'full of greenery, busts, statuettes of angelic faces and monkeys playing instruments'. In this 'oasis', you can 'take a quiet drink after sightseeing'. 'Good breakfast: scrambled eggs and bacon available at extra cost.' 'Our family room was large and comfortable' (children are warmly welcomed). 'Honest good service.' 'Outstandingly helpful desk staff.'

Open All year. **Rooms** 38 double, 6 single. 2 on ground floor. **Facilities** Lift. Lounge, breakfast room. Courtyard garden with bar. **Location** 300 m W of St Mark's Square. **Credit cards** All major cards accepted. **Terms** B&B: single €100–€180, double €130–€230.

LOCANDA CIPRIANI   romantic

Piazza Santa Fosca 29   *Tel* 00 39 041 730150
Torcello   *Fax* 00 39 041 735433
30012 Venezia   *Email* info@locandacipriani.com
                                Website www.locandacipriani.com

The little island of Torcello, 45 minutes by *vaporetto* from
Venice, attracts many visitors for lunch at the Cipriani
family's 'sophisticated and romantic' restaurant in 'lovely,
well-tended gardens'. It has two large dining rooms and a
terrace. There are Venetian bas-reliefs, and old copper pots
are dotted round. The bar has a wood fire in winter. At
night, residents have Torcello for themselves when they stay
in the rustic-style rooms (with wooden ceiling and
terracotta bricks) above the restaurant. Recent visitors liked
the 'gloriously faded feel': pictures of Hemingway, old prints
of Torcello, and a creaky wooden floor upstairs. 'Our super
room, Concordia, looked over the gardens to the church:
cream walls and furniture, loads of books in various
languages, flowers, bathrobes in the lilac mosaic-tiled
bathroom. They'd done 150 Sunday lunches, but the place
was spotless, and at night we were there with one other
couple. Dinner was decent if not great.' Breakfast, under the
trellis, includes 'excellent blood orange juice, lovely almond
and jam croissants, nice coffee and chocolate'.

Open 10 Feb–5 Jan. Restaurant closed Tues to non-residents.
Rooms 1 suite, 2 junior suites, 3 single. No TV. **Facilities** Bar,
restaurant. Garden (meal service). **Location** Island in Lagoon of
Venice. 10 mins' walk from water-bus stop. **Credit cards** All
major cards accepted. **Terms** B&B €120–€170; D,B&B €170–€220.

VERONA/BRESCIA
(Ryanair)

Ryanair flies to Brescia Montichiari airport,
18 km south of Brescia. It is well placed for
Lake Garda and is 50 km from Verona.

HOTEL TORCOLO
charm

Vicolo Listone 3
37121 Verona

Tel 00 39 045 8007512
Fax 00 39 045 8004058
Email hoteltorcolo@virgilio.it
Website www.hoteltorcolo.it

Near Verona's historic arena, this simple B&B, owned by
Silvia Pomari and her sister, Diana, 'offers personal service',
according to visitors. 'Excellent', 'charming' are other
comments. The bedrooms (some are in the cheaper
annexe) vary in size; they have 'interesting furniture',
minibar and safe. All have double glazing, but some traffic
noise can penetrate. 'Enjoyable breakfasts' are served on
the roadside terrace, or in a tiny room with prints of
Verona. No restaurant, but the cafés of Piazza Bra are close
by (Verona's *Torcolo* restaurant has no connection with this
hotel). Taking a car into Verona is 'nightmarish', but the
Torcolo has a street-parking concession and an arrangement
with a local garage.

Open All year, except 7 Jan–7 Feb. **Rooms** 15 double, 4 single.
Facilities Lift. Breakfast room; terrace. **Location** Central, off
Piazza Bra, near arena. Parking. **Credit cards** All major cards
accepted. **Terms** Room: single €48–€75, double €70–€108.
Breakfast €11.

VILLA DEL SOGNO   lakeside

Via Zanardelli 107
Gardone Riviera
25083 Brescia

Tel 00 39 0365 290181
Fax 00 39 0365 290230
Email info@villadelsogno.it
Website www.villadelsogno.it

'A lovely place to stay': on the shore of Lake Garda, the Calderan family's yellow mansion was built by a Viennese silk merchant in 1904. 'Everything was first class; standards of housekeeping were high,' says a recent visitor. Reached up a steep winding road, it has 'magnificent interiors and paintings, bags of atmosphere'. The 'lovely' large public rooms have flowery padded chairs, oriental rugs, wood panelling, majolica and statuary. In the gardens are lemon and olive trees, cypresses, sculptures and an abundance of flowers. Almost all bedrooms share the 'wonderful view': some have a balcony. 'Our room, though small, was beautifully decorated.' Another was 'large, with every comfort'. 'The staff are friendly.' On warm days, guests eat on the flowery lakeside terrace. The cooking, 'international rather than Italian', is mostly enjoyed. 'Excellent breakfast: plenty of fresh fruit, good bread' ('but canned orange juice'). The 'delightful swimming pool' (with bar) is surrounded by loungers; above it is a 'fine, slightly neglected temple with sensational views'.

Open Apr–Oct. **Rooms** 5 suites, 25 double, 1 single. **Facilities** Lift. 2 lounges, TV room, bar, piano bar, restaurant; fitness room. Large garden: dining terrace. **Location** At Fasano, 1 km NE of Gardone Riviera. Free private parking. **Credit cards** All major cards accepted. **Terms** B&B: single €185–€215, double €260–€450, suite €430–€480. Set dinner €50; full alc €80.

VILLA CORTINE PALACE   luxury

Via Grotte 6   *Tel* 00 39 030 9905890
Sirmione   *Fax* 00 39 030 916390
25019 Brescia   *Email* info@hotelvillacortine.com
                               Website www.hotelvillacortine.com

In a large park above Lake Garda, reached by a 'moderately hair-raising' drive through the town's narrow alleys, crowded in summer, this luxury hotel is an extension to a neo-classical villa built in 1870 as a private residence. It has a Palladian-style façade, and huge public rooms with chandeliers, frescoes and mosaics, and it stands in a beautiful garden, with tall trees, a Neptune fountain and a swimming pool. As it is near the end of the peninsula, it has lake views on both sides. Much praise: 'A most enjoyable stay, an excellent room and friendly staff.' 'Expensive but worth it', 'A haven of peace.' A steep walk down, past Roman ruins, leads to the lake, where, in summer, a buffet lunch is served in a pleasant restaurant. Dinner and breakfast are taken on a large terrace looking over the water. The meals have been considered 'outstanding' . Most bedrooms are in a 1950s extension: almost all have a balcony and lake view. 'Ours was beautiful.'

Open 10 April–19 Oct. **Rooms** 2 suites, 4 junior suites, 48 double. **Facilities** Lift. Salons, bar, restaurant. Park: garden, terrace, beach with bar. **Location** Near Grotto of Catullus. 35 km W of Verona. Parking. **Credit cards** All major cards accepted. **Terms** B&B: double €300–€420, suite €450–€470; D,B&B (obligatory in high season, min. 3 nights): double €430–€680, suite €580–€780.

VILLA DEL QUAR   monumental

Via Quar 12   *Tel* 00 39 045 6800681
Pedemonte   *Fax* 00 39 045 6800604
37020 Verona   *Email* villadelquar@c-point.it
                             Website www.hotelvilladelquar.it

Set among vineyards not far from Verona, the Montresor-Acampora family's luxurious hotel/restaurant (Relais & Châteaux) is a designated national monument: a 16th-century patrician dwelling built over 14th-century foundations. One guest described it as 'the modern Maserati of small Italian hotels', with 'distinctive style and elegance and properly engineered underpinnings'. Many original features remain; furniture is 'antique neo-classical'. Other assets: 'The relaxed location, the neat but darkish bedrooms [some have oak beams and antiques], the public rooms with asymmetrically positioned artefacts, the food' (*Michelin* star for Bruno Barbieri). A wide lawn surrounds the large swimming pool, where a new bar/gazebo has been created. There is a terrace for outdoor dining, and a jogging track in the large grounds. The village has a museum devoted to the Walsers, an ancient religious order who speak a form of old German.

Open 15 Mar–8 Jan. Restaurant closed midday on Mon and Tues Mar/April, Nov/Dec. **Rooms** 2 suites, 2 junior suites, 18 double. **Facilities** Salon, bar, tea room, restaurant; terrace. **Location** 7 km NW of Verona. **Credit cards** All major cards accepted. **Terms** B&B: single €197–€300, double €245–€300, suite €305–€400. Set lunch €50, dinner €70; alc €75.

NETHERLANDS

AMSTERDAM
(bmibaby, easyJet, Jet2)

Schipol airport is 18 km from the city centre.

CANAL HOUSE HOTEL   treasure trove

Keizersgracht 148   *Tel* 00 31 20 622 51 82
1015 CX Amsterdam   *Fax* 00 31 20 624 13 17
                                     Email info@canalhouse.nl
                                     Website www.canalhouse.nl

The 'amiable' Irish owners, Brian and Mary Bennett, run this unassuming B&B in the bohemian Jordaan district. A returning visitor found it 'as good as before'. 'Our quiet room at the back overlooked the garden; tastefully decorated, it had a pretty canopied bed. Our friends' room, higher up, was less charming but the view over the canal made up for this.' The 17th-century house is 'a treasure trove of wax pictures, carved objects, little tapestries, wrought iron, plants and ecclesiastic bric-a-brac'. It is a rambling place, 'not for the infirm'. An 'adequate' breakfast is served in a large garden-facing room. The bar serves tea and drinks.

Open All year. **Rooms** 22 double, 4 single. No TV. **Facilities** Lift. Lounge/bar, breakfast room. Garden: summer house. **Location** Central, near Westerkirk. **Restriction** No children under 12. **Credit cards** All major cards accepted. **Terms** B&B single/double €140–€190.

AMBASSADE HOTEL   favourite

Herengracht 341   *Tel* 00 31 20 555 02 22
1016 AZ Amsterdam   *Fax* 00 31 20 555 02 77
                         Email info@ambassade-hotel.nl
                         Website www.ambassade-hotel.nl

'Not hotel-like at all, though the amenities are there; more like being a guest in a house.' 'Delightful. Large, comfortable bedroom, excellent breakfasts.' Praise from visitors to this long-time favourite, a B&B hotel spread among ten 17th-century gabled houses on two of the city's finest canals, the Herengracht and the Singel. Owned by Mr W Schopman, it is 'thoughtfully run' by Ireen Wyers and Dick Westerneng: they provide umbrellas by the door, city maps, bicycle hire, help with restaurants (*Tempo Doloe*, Indonesian, is liked). The 'attentive staff' are 'good at meeting requests for extra glasses, pillows, etc'. Public rooms have tall windows, crystal chandeliers, clocks and paintings. 'The period sitting room is charming.' Bedrooms, varying in size according to altitude, are in period or modern Dutch style. Front ones can get street noise. Most bedrooms 'are up or down a few steps' and the room where the 'plentiful breakfast' is served from 7 until 11 am (11.30 at the weekend) is 'reached by a narrow flight of stairs'.

Open All year. **Rooms** 8 suites, 50 double, 1 single. 5 in annexe. **Facilities** Lifts. Lobby, 2 lounges, breakfast room; library, Internet facility. **Location** Central. **Credit cards** All major cards accepted. **Terms** Room: single €158–€165, double €188–€195, suite €260–€340. Breakfast €16.

HOTEL DE L'EUROPE fin de siècle

Nieuwe Doelenstraat 2–8 *Tel* 00 31 20 531 17 77
1012 CP Amsterdam *Fax* 00 31 20 531 17 78
Email hotel@leurope.nl
Website www.leurope.nl

At the confluence of two canals and the river Amstel ('the best location in Amsterdam,' an enthusiastic visitor wrote), this imposing Victorian hotel is 'very expensive, but it has good service and great food'. Managed by Adriaan Grandia, it has been described as 'a happy mix of a large hotel of character and the kind of ambience that goes with family ownership'. The public rooms are grand: a *fin de siècle* lounge has a collection of Dutch landscapes. There is a canalside café, a bar, *Freddy's*, a gourmet restaurant, *Excelsior* (with a French chef, Jean-Jacques Menanteau), and a brasserie, *Le Relais*. Many other good restaurants are near. Some bedrooms have a balcony and windows opening on to the canal; quietest rooms overlook the courtyard. A new air-conditioning system has been installed – and new lifts. The American breakfast is found 'splendid'. The fitness centre has a gym and a 'small but useful' Grecian-style swimming pool. Nearby are Rembrandt's house, the Rijksmuseum and the flower market.

Open All year. *Excelsior* restaurant closed 1–7 Jan, Sat midday, Sun midday. **Rooms** 6 suites, 17 junior suites, 56 double, 21 single. **Facilities** Lift, ramp. Lounge, café, bar, restaurant; brasserie. Riverside terrace. **Location** Central, opposite flower market. Garage. **Credit cards** All major cards accepted. **Terms** Room: single €285, double €350, suite €455–€990. Breakfast €25. Set lunch €47.50, dinner €70; full alc €85.

EINDHOVEN
(Ryanair)

The airport is to the west of Eindhoven.

DE SWAEN	17th-century inn

De Lind 47
5601 HT Oisterwijk

Tel 00 31 13 523 32 33
Fax 00 31 13 528 58 60
Email swaen@swaen.nl
Website www.slh.com/swaen

A 'beautifully restored' 17th-century inn on the quiet main street of this picturesque town, 'with old houses and nice shops', some 25 km north-west of Eindhoven. 'A lovely old-fashioned hotel, very special,' says one visitor. 'Our elegant front room had a big balcony: a great place for a nightcap. The bathroom was grand, in marble, with gold taps. We had a superb meal in the *Michelin*-starred restaurant, which overlooks a large walled garden with a small pond': meals are taken outdoors in summer. There is also a brasserie, *De Jonge Swaen*: breakfast is served here, and was found 'disappointing'; a buffet with rolls, cereals and fruit but 'half-cold coffee' from a Thermos.

Open All year, except 2 weeks in July. Restaurant closed Sun, Mon. **Rooms** 2 suites, 22 double. **Facilities** 2 restaurants, bar. Terrace, garden. **Location** Central, on main street. Parking. **Credit cards** All major cards accepted. **Terms** Room €135–€165. Breakfast €17. Set lunch €29, dinner €48–€99; full alc €82.

GRONINGEN
(Ryanair)

The airport is just to the south of this historic town.

SCHIMMELPENNINCK HUYS   patrician

Oosterstraat 53
9711 NR Groningen

Tel 00 31 50 318 95 02
Fax 00 31 50 318 31 64
Email info@schimmelpenninckhuys.nl
Website www.schimmelpenninckhuys.nl

The Greek-Dutch Karistinos-Smit family have rescued this patrician's house, near the market square of mainly traffic-free old Groningen, from squatters and developers. They are 'much in evidence', 'proud of their creation'. 'A great hotel; difficult to find, but worth it once you do,' says a visitor. The 'very grand' lounge is decorated in *Jugendstil*. The bedrooms, which vary in size, are in five buildings around the leafy courtyard where meals are served in fine weather. The *Parelvisser* restaurant, in a building across the garden, specialises in seafood; the *Classique*, in an 18th-century room in the front of the house, is traditional French. A recent comment: 'Good ambience, good food, a wonderful welcome, and the staff are friendly.'

Open All year. **Rooms** 6 suites, 43 double, 3 single. **Facilities** Lounge, café, 2 restaurants. Courtyard garden. **Location** Central, off Grote Markt. Public car park 2 blocks away. **Credit cards** Amex, MasterCard, Visa. **Terms** Room: single €50–€75, double €85–€115, suite €150. Breakfast €12. Set lunch €27.50, dinner €37.50; full alc €45.

NORWAY

OSLO
(Ryanair)

Ryanair flies to Sandefjord airport Torp,
110 km south-west of Oslo.

GABELSHUS HOTEL character

Gabelsgate 16
0272 Oslo

Tel 00 47 23 27 65 00
Fax 00 47 23 27 65 60
Email booking@gabelshus.no
Website www.gabelshus.no

In the leafy embassy area, away from traffic noise, this *Historiske Hotel* member is endorsed by two recent guests: 'Very, very nice.' 'Very fine accommodation.' The 'lovely old building' is a 'welcoming hotel of character'. The 'wonderful' public rooms are 'old-style Norwegian': carved wooden furniture, wood panelling, shining copper and brass, and clocks. The buffet dinner is 'delicious and good value'. Most bedrooms are spacious; some have a sitting area. 'My large double had huge bed, sofa and chairs, antiques and polished wooden floors. Its white bathroom was spacious.' A breakfast buffet table is laden with cereals, cheese, cold meats, bread and yogurt. Tea, coffee and waffles are available all day.

Open All year, except Christmas/New Year, Easter. **Rooms** 1 suite, 28 double, 14 single. **Facilities** Bar, 2 lounges, restaurant. Garden, terrace. **Location** W side of city, between Bygdøy Alley and Drammensv. Bus/tram nearby. **Credit cards** All major cards accepted. **Terms** B&B: single 750–1,295 Nkr, double 950–1,495 Nkr, suite 1,790 Nkr.

PORTUGAL

FARO

(bmibaby, easyJet, FlyBE, Jet2, MyTravelLite)

Faro airport is 5 km west of the city.

MONTE DO CASAL
tranquil

Cerro do Lobo
Estoi
8005-436 Algarve

Tel 00 351 289 99 15 03
Fax 00 351 289 99 13 41
Email montedocasal@mail.telepac.pt
Website www.montedocasal.pt

Owner/chef Bill Hawkins has converted this 18th-century farmhouse, on the edge of a 13th-century market town north-east of Faro, into a small luxury hotel/restaurant. In the large grounds (floodlit at night) are bougainvillaea, almond, olive and fruit trees, two swimming pools, two waterfalls, rock pools and a stream. The emphasis is on tranquillity: children under 16 are admitted only during two weeks in July. Much liked are the rooms with a sea-facing terrace, where the continental breakfast, 'subtly varied from day to day', can be taken. Six rooms are in the gardens. Guests dine by candlelight, alfresco or in a converted coach house. Estoi is well placed for exploring the eastern Algarve.

Open Early Feb–20 Nov. **Rooms** 5 suites, 14 double. **Facilities** 2 lounges, bar, restaurant. **Location** 3 km NE of Estoi, *c.* 10 km NE of Faro. **Credit cards** Amex, MasterCard, Visa. **Terms** B&B: single €97–€193.50, double €129–€258, suite €168–€300. Set Sun lunch €25, dinner €44; full alc €65.

CASA TRÊS PALMEIRAS   dream setting

Apartado 84

Praia do Vau

8501-909 Algarve

Tel 00 351 282 40 12 75

Fax 00 351 282 40 10 29

Email dolly@casatrespalmeiras.com

Website www.casatrespalmeiras.com

An upmarket B&B in a 'dream setting' on a cliff edge, near Portimão, in the western Algarve. It has 'incomparable views of sea, sky, rocks, beach and the sweep of the bay'. The 'charming' multilingual Brazilian owner, Dolly Schlingensiepen, is 'a caring hostess, you feel quietly pampered', says a fan. Just five bedrooms: they are 'of the highest quality, spotless, with spacious, superb beds, fridge, fruit, satellite TV'. Each is allotted a space by the small fish-shaped sea-water swimming pool on the terrace which four bedrooms face; the fifth room has its own large terrace and a garden view. A path leads to a quiet, sandy beach. Breakfast, ordered the night before, and served after 8.30 am, includes fresh juice, eggs, bacon, etc. Light lunches are available, and advice is given on where to dine. No credit cards: a 40% deposit is required on booking, a further 40% two months before arrival. Difficult to find: ask for directions.

Open Feb–Nov. Rooms 5 double. **Facilities** Lounge with honesty bar. Terrace. Garden: solar-heated swimming pool. Beach 2 mins' walk. **Location** 4 km from Portimão, 62 km W of Faro airport. Directions provided. **Credit cards** None accepted. **Terms** B&B: single €136–€178, double €160–€200.

QUINTA DA LUA   rustic

Bernardinheiro 1622-X   *Tel/Fax* 00 351 281 96 10 70
Santo Estevão   *Email* quintadalua@quintadalua.com.pt
8800-513 Faro   *Website* www.quintadalua.com.pt

Near Tavira, in a rural area of the eastern Algarve north-east of Faro ('away from the golfing belt'), this small hotel, owned and managed by Miguel Martins and Vimal Willems, is set amid orange trees and vineyards. Recently discovered by regular *Good Hotel Guide* correspondents, who wrote: 'Very quiet, and very well run', it has 'comfortable if not over-large rooms in rustic style'. A 'superb breakfast' (fresh fruit, cakes and jam, local cheeses, excellent coffee) is served on the terrace, and there is an honesty bar and a barbecue. A simple meal is sometimes served to residents by arrangement. The garden has shady sitting areas, and an 'ecological' saltwater pool. 'The orange blossom and herb scents were lovely. A great place for hill-walkers.' The sea, with long sandy beaches, is ten minutes' drive away.

Open 15 Dec–15 Nov. **Rooms** 2 suites (with TV), 6 double. **Facilities** Dining room. 2-hectare garden: terrace. **Location** 25 km NE of Faro, 4 km NW of Tavira. Santo Estevão turning off EN125 from Faro. 1st left, 1st right. Look for gateway arch. **Restrictions** No children. No smoking. **Credit cards** None accepted. **Terms** B&B: single €45–€80, double €55–€90, suite €75–€120. Set lunch €12.50, dinner €20.

SPAIN

ALICANTE
(bmibaby, easyJet, FlyBE, Jet2, MyTravelLite)

El Altet airport is 11 km south of Alicante.

CASA DEL MACO   rustic

Pou Roig   *Tel* 00 34 965 73 28 42
Benissa   *Fax* 00 34 965 73 01 03
03720 Alicante   *Email* macomarcus@hotmail.com
                                   Website www.casadelmaco.com

An 18th-century farmhouse, white-walled and tile-roofed, which stands in terraced gardens, amid vineyards, olive groves and almond orchards, on a ridge in the Lleus valley, 37 km north of Benidorm. A Flemish photographer, Bert de Vooght, has turned it into a small rustic hotel/restaurant. It is warmly recommended: 'Outstanding: homely, with a welcoming atmosphere, delightful staff.' The 'comfortable, well-equipped' bedrooms have antique furniture; some are beamed. 'The restaurant provides real gourmet fare, and breakfast is a delight, with home-baked breads, fresh orange juice, excellent cheese and ham.' Meals are served on a patio on fine days; herbs for the kitchen are grown by the swimming pool.

Open All year, except Jan. Restaurant closed Tues. **Rooms** 6 double. **Facilities** Lounge, restaurant. Terrace. Garden. **Location**. From N332 Calpe–Benissa, take small road on left 1 km after petrol station. Follow signs. **Credit cards** All major cards accepted. **Terms** Room: single €54–€87, double €66–€99. Breakfast €9. D,B&B €69–€123 per person.

HOTEL EL MONTÍBOLI   luxury

Partida el Montíboli s/n   *Tel* 00 34 965 89 02 50
Villajoyosa   *Fax* 00 34 965 89 38 57
03570 Alicante   *Email* montiboli@servigroup.es
                              Website www.servigroup.es

'An upmarket hideaway' (Relais & Châteaux), built like a
traditional village with Moorish gardens, in a glorious cliff-top
setting above the sea, near Alicante. A recent visitor found it
'an escape from an otherwise spoilt coastline'. There are
twisting walkways – 'lots of steps between the buildings'. The
ambience is 'discreet', the service 'friendly'. The decor is
attractive: beamed ceilings, stone walls, period furniture.
Bedrooms vary: 'Newer ones, below the entrance level, are
best'; 'ask for a room with a sea view' (and avoid one near
the air-conditioning unit). The pool sun deck has 'great
views'; two 'nice, if stony' small beaches down steep steps,
with loungers, have parasols and a bar/restaurant. 'Copious'
buffet breakfast.

Open All year. **Rooms** 12 suites, 38 double. **Facilities** TV
lounge, bar, 2 restaurants. Large garden: 3 swimming pools.
Location 3 km SW of Villajoyosa on Alicante road. Parking.
Credit cards All major cards accepted. **Terms** B&B €70–€180.
Set meal €37; full alc €60.

ALMERÍA
(MyTravelLite)

The airport is just to the east of Almería.

ALQUERÍA DE MORAYMA   **farmstay**

Alpujarra   *Tel/Fax* 00 34 958 34 32 21
Cádiar   *Email* alqueria@alqueriamorayma.com
18440 Granada   *Website* www.alqueriamorayma.com

In a *pueblo* in the foothills of the Alpujarras, 80-km north west of Almería, this *centro agri-turístico*, with 'splendid views', is run by Mariano Cruz Fajardo. A 'down-to-earth place', it is a collection of buildings on an organic farm with vineyards, an olive grove and orchards. Guests are encouraged to take part, 'picking fruit, making sausages'. One wrote: 'It is memorable for the rural setting, and the charm and friendliness of the staff. A good area for walking, followed by delicious, authentic Spanish food in the evening.' The decor is in local style: white walls, beamed ceilings. Bedrooms may be rustic, but bathrooms are modern. Breakfast, on the 'delightful grassy terrace', has fresh orange juice, toast, honey and good coffee.

Open All year. **Rooms** 4 suites, 14 double. In 18 units (some self-catering). **Facilities** Library, bar, restaurant. 38-hectare farm: garden, unheated swimming pool. **Location** 3 km SW of Cádiar, on road to Torvizcón; 85 km SE of Granada. **Credit cards** MasterCard, Visa. **Terms** Room: single €48, double €59, suite €63. Breakfast €3. Set meals €12.

HOTEL TARAY   peaceful

Carretera A348   *Tel* 00 34 958 78 45 25
Órgiva   *Fax* 00 34 958 78 45 31
18400 Granada   *Email* tarayalp@teleline.es
                        Website www.turgranada.com/hoteltaray

A modern hotel, built in local style, beside the Guadalfeo river, outside a small market town in the mountains between Almería and Granada. 'What joy to wake up with the Alpujarras to the south, and the snow-capped peak of the Sierra Nevada to the north,' said a visitor. 'The hotel was spotless, the rooms well heated for the cold nights.' The owner/manager, Eladio Cuadros, 'is a delight', said others, though one dissenting visitor, in winter, was disappointed with food and service. The 'delightful garden', filled with citrus trees, has a large swimming pool and a pond. 'The peace was disturbed only by birds, an occasional cockerel or mule.' The food is generally thought 'straightforward and satisfying', with lots of local produce, 'discreet, friendly service'. 'The set menu is excellent value.' Breakfast, 'an ample buffet', has freshly squeezed orange juice, home-made jam, eggs, cheese and much else. The simple bungalow-type bedrooms (some call them 'austere') lead on to the lawn. Some have a sitting room, some a private terrace.

Open All year. **Rooms** 3 suites, 3 mini-suites, 9 double. In 2 annexes. **Facilities** Ramps. Reading/music/TV room, bar, restaurant. **Location** 1.5 km from Órgiva, 100 km NW of Almería. Parking. **Credit cards** All major cards accepted. **Terms** Room: single €61, double €65, suite €93. Breakfast €5. Set meals €12.

BARCELONA

(bmibaby, easyJet, Jet2, MyTravelLite, Ryanair)

Barcelona airport is 12 km south of the city.
Ryanair flies to Girona, 80 km north, and
Reus 80 km south.

HOTEL ALEXANDRA   elegant

Carrer Mallorca 251   *Tel* 00 34 93 467 71 66
Barcelona 08008   *Fax* 00 34 93 488 02 58
                          Email informacion@hotel-alexandra.com
                          Website www.hotel-alexandra.com

A large, elegant, modern hotel, well located between Passeig
de Gràcia (where you can see La Pedrera, Gaudí's unusual
apartment building without a single straight line) and La
Rambla. 'It offers a comfortable base at a reasonable price
for the location,' says a regular visitor. 'Rooms, decorated in
brown-beige marble, vary in size, but are generally big with a
good bathroom. Some fittings (wobbly tabletops, loose
cupboard doors) occasionally let down the design.
Reception staff are helpful, and there is a pleasant mezzanine
bar.'

Open All year. **Rooms** 8 suites, 91 double. **Facilities** Lobby, bar,
restaurant; shops. **Location** Central, between Passeig de Gràcia
and Rambla de Catalunya. **Credit cards** All major cards accepted.
Terms Room: single €155–€225, double €185–€290, suite
€310–€450. Breakfast €16. Set meals €20.

HOTEL CLARIS   designer

Pau Claris 150   *Tel* 00 34 93 487 62 62
Barcelona 08009   *Fax* 00 34 93 215 79 70
                                        Email claris@derbyhotels.es
                                        Website www.derbyhotels.es

The neo-classical façade of the 19th-century Palacio Vedruna is set into 'a modern edifice of dark glass', behind which stands this designer hotel *gran luxe* in the Eixample district, near the city's best shopping. Inside is an 'uncompromisingly contemporary' decor: lifts rise above an atrium to glass and marble galleries leading to the bedrooms. Sculptures, paintings and antique kilim rugs are distributed throughout, and there is a small museum of Egyptian artefacts. Recent praise: 'Courteous staff; not a trace of coldness.' 'Marvellous; they really look after you.' 'The cool modern style continues in the bedrooms: beautiful wooden cupboards and panelling.' 'Our quiet room was small but perfectly turned out: powerful reading lights, a luxurious bathroom. We slept with the window open.' Three restaurants: *Terraza del Claris*, on the rooftop terrace by the swimming pool, has a glass ceiling; *East 47*, hung with Warhol lithographs, serves 'excellent creative cuisine'; *Claris* is for local specialities. 'First-rate buffet breakfast in a pleasant basement room.' 'Unabashedly pricey, but we found a good rate on the Internet.'

Open All year. *Terraza* restaurant open June–Oct. **Rooms** 39 suites, 81 double, 4 single. **Facilities** Bar, 3 restaurants. **Location** Central. (Metro: Passeig de Gràcia) **Credit cards** All major cards accepted. **Terms** Room: single up to €335, double up to €372, suite up to €946. Breakfast €19. Full alc €170.

HOTEL SANT AUGUSTÍ   value

Plaça Sant Augustí 3
Barcelona 08001

Tel 00 34 93 318 16 58
Fax 00 34 93 317 29 28
Email hotelsa@hotelsa.com
Website www.hotelsa.com

Also called *Hotel San Augustín*, this former convent claims to be the oldest hotel in the city. Next to the Liceu opera house, in a square just off La Rambla, it offers 'simple, comfortable accommodation and good value', say visitors. 'Staff are friendly. Our back room, recently decorated, was pleasantly cool, thanks to air-conditioning. It had wooden floors, lots of storage space, a safe, excellent marble bathroom, really hot water. Some corridor noise, not troublesome.' From the front rooms you might hear late-night revellers. 'Breakfast, overlooking the square, had fresh baguettes and rolls, a toasting machine, good coffee, but packaged orange juice, alas.' The restaurant serves Catalan dishes, but you could join the Spanish for 'traditional food at incredible prices' at the €7 three-course lunch at *Les Quinze Nits,* in nearby Plaça Real.

Open All year. **Rooms** 75. **Facilities** Lift. Lounge, lobby, bar, restaurant, background music. Free Internet connection. **Location** 100 m off Las Ramblas at Calle Hospital. (Metro: Liceu). **Credit cards** All major cards accepted. **Terms** B&B: single €95–€132, double €126–€158.

BILBAO
(easyJet)

The airport is close to the town.

ITURRIENEA OSTATUA   budget

Santa María Kalea 14   *Tel* 00 34 94 416 15 00
Bilbao 48005   *Fax* 00 34 94 415 89 29

A simple *pension*, near the cathedral and the lively *Mercado de la Ribera* in the *casco viejo*, that remains ever-popular for its 'amazing value', and for the breakfast, apart from the orange juice ('vast pastries, luscious bread, figs, etc'), which goes on until noon. 'Delightful.' 'Everything you need, nothing you don't,' say enthusiasts. Basque paintings hang on the walls. The public rooms, 'dotted with an eccentric collection of curios', are found 'cluttered' by some, and from some street-facing rooms revellers can be heard at weekends. The bedrooms, 'with old beams and interesting antique furniture', are 'small but cleverly put together'. There is a little patio with potted plants. The Guggenheim is a short journey away by the 'smart, incredibly cheap' Metro.

Open All year. **Rooms** 14 double, 7 single. **Facilities** Breakfast room. Small patio. **Location** Old town, near river. **Credit cards** Diners, MasterCard, Visa. **Terms** Room: single €45, double €57. Breakfast €3.

LÓPEZ DE HARO   luxury

Obispo Orueta 2–4   *Tel* 00 34 94 423 55 00
Bilbao 48009   *Fax* 00 34 94 423 45 00
                              Email lh@hotellopezdeharo.com
                              Website www.hotellopezdeharo.com

Efficiently run, with 'well-appointed rooms', this 'very nice' luxury hotel, owned by the Ercilla group, is near the Guggenheim museum and the attractive pedestrian areas. One couple, visiting at a quiet time, thought it 'lacked that spark that makes a place special', but everyone agrees that the staff are 'very helpful'. It has marble floors, oriental rugs, trailing plants in public rooms. 'Our quiet suite was large, with an even larger bathroom.' 'Our room was small, but perfectly comfortable.' Some bedrooms are for women only. Guests can choose the type of pillow they want, and they have access to nearby gyms. The small *Club Náutico* restaurant specialises in Basque dishes – 'tapas-style, light and good', but a bar meal was found disappointing. *Zortziko*, one of Bilbao's three *Michelin*-starred restaurants, is round the corner. 'Good buffet breakfast, with fresh orange juice.' Special rates, including admission to the Guggenheim, are offered.

Open All year, restaurant closed 1–15 Aug. **Rooms** 4 suites, 35 double, 14 single. **Facilities** Lift. 3 salons, snack bar, tea room, 2 restaurants. **Location** City centre, near Gran Via and river. **Credit cards** All major cards accepted. **Terms** Room: single €96–€156, double €126–€205, suite €172–€332. Breakfast €11.50. Set meals €30; full alc €50.

GIRONA
(Ryanair)

The airport is 12 km south of the town.

HOTEL RESTAURANT CAN BARRINA   budget

Carretera Palautordera
Montseny
08640 Barcelona

Tel 00 34 93 847 30 65
Fax 00 34 93 847 31 84
Email canbarrina@ctv.es
Website www.canbarrina.com

A restaurant-with-rooms in a converted 17th-century farmhouse, in the mountains between Girona and Barcelona. It has a 'wonderful setting' with 'spectacular views' across the Montseny national park. These can be enjoyed from the terrace where the 'hearty Catalan' cooking, using local fish, mountain raspberries, etc, is served. There is also a rustic dining room. 'Friendly, comfortable, excellent service,' was one recent verdict. 'The food is the thing,' was another. But one visitor disliked the piped music during dinner. Bedrooms range from 'large and high-ceilinged, with a view over the gardens' to 'small but comfortable'. An 'especially good' breakfast is taken on warm days under vines by the 'very attractive pool'. Popular for weddings.

Open All year, except 15 days over Christmas. **Rooms** 14 double. **Facilities** Restaurant. Terrace: swimming pool. **Location** A7 exit 11; left after toll on to C251 towards Granollers, right on to BV5301 towards Santa María Palautordera/Montseny. **Credit cards** Diners, MasterCard, Visa. **Terms** Room: single €60, double €93. Breakfast €9.50. D,B&B €84 per person.

HOTEL RESTAURANT LLEVANT   seaside

Francesc de Blanes 5   *Tel* 00 34 972 30 03 66
Llafranc   *Fax* 00 34 972 30 03 45
17211 Girona   *Email* hllevant@arrakis.es

The Farrarons family's hotel stands on the beach in a small Costa Brava resort, 40 km south-east of Girona. 'Outwardly it is unimpressive,' say returning visitors. 'Inside all is stylish. The bedrooms are light, well furnished, with lovely wood floors, good beds and linen. Street noise can be a problem in some rooms [the best ones, looking over the sea, are hard to get], but the owners and their dedicated staff make up for this.' Another visitor was reminded by her 'beautifully appointed room' of 'a luxury yacht'. Bedrooms vary in size: medium to quite small. In the 'immaculate' dining room (with white tablecloths on ranks of tables) facing the sea, or on the attractive dining terrace, there is always fresh fish on the daily-changing *table d'hôte* dinner menu. 'The turbot was so good, we had it twice.' But another visitor thought the food 'nondescript'. 'The beach can be crowded in high season, but the village was quiet in June; a lovely unspoilt spot on a beautiful coastline.'

Open All year, except Nov. **Rooms** 20 double, 4 single. **Facilities** Lift. 2 lounges, bar, restaurant. Terrace. **Location** Seafront of village. 5 km SE of Palafrugell. **Credit cards** Amex, MasterCard, Visa. **Terms** B&B (low season only): single €38–€48, double €63–€90; D,B&B: single €60–€125, double €106–€203.

JEREZ
(Ryanair)

The airport is 5 km north of Jerez.

VILLA JEREZ
luxury

Avenida de la Cruz Roja 7
Jerez de la Frontera
11407 Cádiz

Tel 00 34 956 15 31 00
Fax 00 34 956 30 43 00
Email reservas@villajerez.com
Website www.villajerez.com

This old mansion, in an appealing part of town, was recently converted into a luxury hotel. 'Expensive but worth it,' says a visitor. 'Most relaxing. Very quiet for a city-centre hotel: we slept with the windows open, and heard owls at night, birdsong in the morning.' The rooms are all different: 'Ours, beautifully furnished, had a luxurious bathroom with lots of goodies. The charming staff were attentive, the meals were excellent.' Many bedrooms look over the 'well-maintained' gardens and 'delightful' swimming pool. In this attractive small city (it gave its name to sherry), there is much to see: visit one of the sherry *bodegas*, or the famous Royal Andalusian School of Equestrian Art.

Open All year. **Rooms** 4 suites, 12 double, 2 single. **Facilities** Lift. Reading room, bar, restaurant. **Location** Central, off Plaza del Caballo. Parking, garage. **Credit cards** All major cards accepted. **Terms** B&B: single €207–€236, double €272–€309, suite €330–€403. Set meals €31; full alc €48.

HOTEL EL CONVENTO   budget

Calle Maldonado 2
Arcos de la Frontera
11630 Cádiz

Tel 00 34 956 70 23 33
Fax 00 34 956 70 41 28
Email hotelelconvento@terra.es
Website www.webdearcos.com/elconvento

Arcos de la Frontera is a historic town of whitewashed houses, 24 km east of Jerez, built on a steep hill with spectacular views over the plain of the Guadelete. In a traffic-free street at the top of the hill is the Moreno family's converted convent, which offers a cheaper alternative to the nearby *parador*. Visitors find it 'delightful', with 'most helpful' staff. The famous view can be enjoyed from some bedrooms, and from the rooftop sun terrace. Some bedrooms are small; and a bed's foot-boards caused some discomfort to one six-foot-four-inch visitor. The restaurant, in the arcaded covered patio of a nearby 17th-century palace, has a *Michelin Bib Gourmand* for its regional cooking, eg, convent soup (with onion, cheese and walnuts). The family also own the 19-room *Los Olivos del Convento*, a conversion of old houses around a courtyard, down the hill.

Open All year, except 2 weeks Jan, 1 week July. **Rooms** 10 double, 1 single. **Facilities** Breakfast room/bar, restaurant. Roof terrace. **Location** Top of town; follow directions to *parador*. Park in Plaza del Cabildo, take Calle Escribanos: hotel signposted. **Credit cards** All major cards accepted. **Terms** Room: single €35–€55, double €50–€80. Breakfast €5. Set meals €24; full alc €30.

MÁLAGA
(bmibaby, easyJet, FlyBE, Jet2,
MyTravelLite, Thomsonfly)

The airport is 6 km west of Málaga.

REFUGIO DE JUANAR   hunting lodge

Sierra Blanca   *Tel* 00 34 95 288 10 00
Ojén   *Fax* 00 34 95 288 10 01
29610 Málaga   *Email* juanar@sopde.es
                                      Website www.juanar.com

Up a narrow, twisting road behind Marbella, this former aristocratic hunting lodge belongs to an Andalusian association of rural hotels. It is in a nature reserve in the foothills of the Sierra Blanca. 'A popular place,' say visitors, 'very active and enjoyable.' Others found it peaceful, including General de Gaulle, who came here in 1970 to work on his memoirs. The 'warm welcome' is liked; also the 'attractive lounges with log fires', the spacious rustic bedrooms, and the good food. The restaurant, 'jolly with red gingham and local ceramics', is a favourite lunchtime spot for local families. Game is a speciality. The decor has a sporting theme: stuffed pheasants, English hunting scenes. In the large grounds are tennis and a swimming pool.

Open All year. **Rooms** 5 suites, 20 double, 1 single. **Facilities** Lift. 2 salons, TV room, bar, restaurant. **Location** 9 km W of Ojén, off A355 to Ronda by narrow road to left (signposted). **Credit cards** All major cards accepted. **Terms** Room: single €60–€70, double €80–€92, suite €175–€195. Breakfast €7. D,B&B €22 added per person.

LA POSADA DEL TORCAL   country

Partido de Jeva   *Tel* 00 34 952 03 11 77
Villanueva de la Concepcón   *Fax* 00 34 952 03 10 06
29230 Málaga   *Email* posadatorcal@codesat.net
                    Website www.eltorcal.com/posadatorcal

Below the limestone outcrops of El Torcal national park, this small, white, modern hotel, built in local style (ancient beams, antiques and ceramics), has glorious views across almond and olive groves to the rolling Andalusian countryside. All agree that the swimming pool, which enjoys the best views, is 'relaxing and quiet'; chilled drinks are available on an honesty basis from the pool-house bar. The 'caring' manager, Michael Soffe, 'knows the area well'; the staff are 'charming'; a 'delightful' dog, Kippis, takes guests for walks. Bedrooms, each named after a Spanish artist, have a large bed (mattresses are new), a sunken bath, a balcony, and a wood-burning stove. An 'excellent' breakfast ('with fried eggs and local bacon') is taken on a terrace. The restaurant serves an Andalusian menu. Many guests are English. A 25 per cent non-refundable deposit is requested at the time of booking.

Open All year, except Dec/Jan. **Rooms** 1 suite, 9 double. **Facilities** Salon, bar, 2 restaurants. 4-hectare grounds. **Location** 40 km N of Málaga. 3 km from village (signposted). **Credit cards** All major cards accepted. **Terms** (Min. 3 nights Mar–Oct) B&B: single €125, double €155–€180, suite €260. Set meals €35; full alc €42.

PALMA

(Air Berlin, bmibaby, easyJet, Jet2,
MyTravelLite, Thomsonfly)

Palma de Mallorca airport is 11 km south-east
of the city.

HOTEL SAN LORENZO   romantic

Calle San Lorenzo 14	*Tel* 00 34 971 72 82 00
Palma	*Fax* 00 34 971 71 19 01
07012 Mallorca	*Email* info@hotelsanlorenzo.com
	Website www.hotelsanlorenzo.com

In Palma's old quarter, this tall, narrow, 17th-century town house is now a 'very romantic' small luxury hotel. It has been sensitively restored, with wrought iron, tiled floors, beams, potted palms, etc. There is a ground-floor patio, an Art Deco bar in the bar/breakfast room, and a 'beautiful small swimming pool', surrounded by palms and bougainvillaea. The 'excellent' breakfast has fresh orange juice, yogurt, fruit, eggs, and *ensaimada* (flaky pastry). The bedrooms, on the two top floors, have antique furniture, open fireplace and Mallorcan tiles; colours are pure white, soft Mediterranean blues. Two rooms above an alley can be noisy; rear ones have a balcony or terrace facing the cathedral. The manager, Susanne Kress, is 'capable and charming'; her staff are admired, too.

Open All year. **Rooms** 2 junior suites, 4 double. **Facilities** Bar/cafeteria. **Location** Old town. **Credit cards** All major cards accepted. **Terms** Room: double €120–€170, suite €210. Breakfast €8–€10.

SCOTT'S HOTEL   bespoke

Plaza de la Iglesia 12	*Tel* 00 34 971 87 01 00
Binissalem	*Fax* 00 34 971 87 02 67
07350 Mallorca	*Email* reserve@scottshotel.com
	Website www.scottshotel.com

'A jewel; a bespoke, rather than a conventional, hotel,' said a recent visitor to George and Judy Scott's tastefully converted 18th-century house, by the church on the main square of a town in the centre of Mallorca's wine-making area. It's an unusual B&B hotel: 'You tell the Scotts what you want – late breakfast, advice on secret beaches, good off-beat restaurants – and they will arrange it.' Earlier visitors were also enthusiastic: 'Outstanding; run with flair and imagination. Nice touches included a printout at breakfast of daily events such as local markets'. Guests have their own front door key and help themselves to drinks on an honesty basis (tea/coffee-making facilities and a fridge are available). There is a bougainvillaea-filled patio with a small fountain, and a non-chlorinated indoor swimming pool like a Roman spa. Breakfast, served until 11.30 am (on the terrace in summer), is 'good continental'. The Scotts own a bistro, nearby: 'good, if relatively expensive'.

Open All year. **Rooms** 6 suites, 11 double. **Facilities** 2 sitting rooms with self-service drinks, bar with TV, breakfast room. **Location** Town centre. 20 km NE of Palma. Free parking adjacent. **Restriction** No children under 12. **Credit cards** Amex, MasterCard, Visa. **Terms** B&B (min. 2 nights): single €131–€154, double €175–€205, suite €235–€270. Set dinner €23; alc €33–€38.

HOTEL SES ROTGES   gourmet

Calle Rafael Blanes 21   *Tel* 00 34 971 56 31 08
Cala Ratjada   *Fax* 00 34 971 56 43 45
07590 Mallorca   *Email* hotel@sesrotges.com
                                  Website www.sesrotges.com

French owner/chef Gérard Tétard, with his wife, Laurence, runs this admired restaurant-with-rooms (*Michelin* star) in an old creeper-clad mansion on a quiet side street of a small fishing resort, on the north-east tip of Mallorca. A visitor enjoyed the 'excellent food, often eaten in the lovely shady courtyard with potted plants and a guitar player' (on cooler days it is served in the old beamed dining room). 'Superb; welcoming, with impeccable service.' French dishes, with 'first-rate presentation', include scallops and asparagus with truffle dressing; rack of lamb feuilleté. Madame discusses the (no-choice) set menu at breakfast 'and makes amendments as necessary', or you could choose from the more expensive *carte* ('particularly good'). Fresh fish from the port is used; there is a wide range of Spanish wines. Breakfast is 'simple but excellent'. 'Comfortable, clean and well-maintained' bedrooms have attractive rustic furnishings, fresh flowers, a good bathroom. Suites have a small lounge. There's a rooftop terrace with loungers. This pleasant town has a 'lovely harbour, nice beaches, good shops'.

Open Mid-Mar–early Nov. **Rooms** 4 suites, 17 double, 3 single. **Facilities** Salon, TV room, bar, restaurant; terrace (summer meals). **Location** Near centre: on entering, take 3rd right, 1st left. 80 km NE of Palma. Parking. **Credit cards** All major cards accepted. **Terms** Room: single €70, double €90, suite €157. Breakfast €11.50. D,B&B €44 added per person.

HOTEL ES MOLÍ   panoramic

Carretera de Valldemossa   *Tel* 00 34 971 63 90 00
Deyá   *Fax* 00 34 971 63 93 33
07179 Mallorca   *Email* reservas@esmoli.com
                                     Website www.esmoli.com

A much-loved holiday hotel on the outskirts of the famous
hill village: it has 'breathtaking views' across olive terraces to
the sea. 'Difficult to find fault,' says a visitor. 'Our lovely
room had a balcony, but it could have done with more
storage space. Gorgeous garden. Drinks, etc, reasonably
priced. Service excellent throughout.' Visitors returning
after 11 years wrote: 'Even better than we remembered.
Staff genuinely friendly; we were astonished to recognise
many from our previous visits.' 'Super swimming pool,
beautifully kept'; 'plenty of sunbeds' stand among orange and
fig trees. Bathrooms are 'excellent'. 'Our annexe room was
spacious.' 'Our room was small but adequate, spotlessly
clean.' Rooms near the road get traffic noise. 'Breakfast,
dinner and lunch by the pool were all excellent.' The *Ca'n
Quet* restaurant, in a separate building, is also enjoyed. A
minibus takes guests to a private beach for sea bathing.
'Pepe's guided walk each Monday is brilliant.'

Open 23 Apr–30 Oct. Dining room closed midday; *Ca'n Quet*
closed Mon. **Rooms** 3 suites, 76 double, 8 single. **Facilities** Lift.
Lounges, bar, dining room, restaurant. **Location** 500 m from
village centre. 29 km NW of Palma. Parking. **Credit cards** All
major cards accepted. **Terms** B&B: single €122–€145, double
€183–€242, suite €368–€400; D,B&B €109.50–€218 per person.

HOTEL LA MORALEJA   intimate

Cala San Vicenç   *Tel* 00 34 971 53 40 10
07469 Mallorca   *Fax* 00 34 971 53 34 18
                                    Email hotel@lamoraleja.net
                                    Website www.la.moraleja.net

'An absolute joy,' say visitors to this luxurious small hotel, composed of two white villas in a residential area. 'Careful landscaping has made it a peaceful oasis. The atmosphere is intimate but laid-back. It is beautifully furnished and maintained – just the right side of chintz. Thanks to ingenious water features and a cage of cheery canaries, you never hear noise from the road.' Others found the hotel friendly, 'with excellent food, comfort and service'. 'The homely feel is aided by the presence of the family owners at every meal.' The English-speaking staff are 'eager to please'. 'Our large bedroom had a wonderful bathroom and private little terrace looking to the nearby hills.' Unusually for Spain, children under 14 are not welcomed. There are two swimming pools (one heated). Good dinner with six choices of main course, daily specials (booking essential). Breakfast, served outdoors on fine days, is 'excellent', 'impeccably served': comprehensive cold buffet; hot dishes cooked to order; 'best fresh juice ever'. The house is filled with a collection of Spanish paintings.

Open 1 May–31 Oct. **Rooms** 1 suite, 15 double, 1 single. **Facilities** Lift, ramps. 2 salons, 2 writing rooms, bar, breakfast room, restaurant. Garden: terraces. **Location** 1 km inland from centre. 10 km NE of Pollensa. **Credit cards** Amex, MasterCard, Visa. **Terms** (Min. 3 nights) B&B: single €201, double €252, suite €321. Full alc €50 to €100.

GRAN HOTEL SON NET

luxury

Castillo Son Net
Puigpunyent
07194 Mallorca

Tel 00 34 971 14 70 00
Fax 00 34 971 14 70 01
Email recepcion@sonnet.es
Website www.sonnet.es

David Stein has filled his 'stunning' conversion of a 17th-century palace (Relais & Châteaux) with original paintings by Warhol, Chagall and Hockney, and works by Spanish classical masters. Painted bright pink, it stands on a small hill amid pine and fruit trees in the Tramuntana mountains, in the south-west of the island. The manager is Carlos Batista. A 'magical' 100-foot swimming pool, surrounded by palm trees and rose bushes, has views to the olive groves below; hedges give sunbathers privacy. There are sculptures in the grounds; the sunsets are spectacular. Recent visitors 'liked the hotel a lot'. Earlier praise: 'Wonderful: fantastic room with a bathroom to die for. Attentive service, very relaxing.' 'Our sumptuous suite had an enormous sitting room and 14-foot-high ceilings.' The restaurant, in an old oil press, serves Mediterranean cuisine ('good value considering the surroundings'): meals can be taken on a terrace or in a courtyard. In summer, there is a grill with bar by the pool. A lavish tea is served in the lounge in winter. 'Good buffet breakfast.'

Open All year. **Rooms** 7 suites, 17 double. **Facilities** Lift. Lounges, restaurant; gym, sauna, whirlpool. Garden. Beaches 15 km. **Location** 400 m NW of village. 12 km NW of Palma. **Credit cards** All major cards accepted. **Terms** Room €199–€420, suite €590–€990. Breakfast €19. Full alc €50–€60.

TENERIFE
(MyTravelLite)

MyTravelLite flies to Reina Sofia airport in the
south. We recommend hotels in the interior
and the north-west of the island.

PARADOR DE CAÑADAS DEL TEIDE   moonscape

Apartado 15, La Orotava	*Tel* 00 34 922 38 64 15
Las Cañadas del Teide	*Fax* 00 34 922 38 23 52
38300 Tenerife	*Email* canadas@parador.es
Canary Islands	*Website* www.parador.es

The only building within Tenerife's moonscape Cañadas del
Teide national park, 2,000 metres above sea level, this
purpose-built *parador* is liked for its 'exceptional value' and
'excellent' food. The low mountain lodge has dark wood
interiors; the lounge/bar has a large open fire, big sofas and
Spanish newspapers; bedrooms are 'stark in the Spanish
fashion'. 'Ours had enormous bed; brightly lit bathroom with
marble floor and eccentric shower.' Dinner has a
Canarian/cosmopolitan menu: 'Take the rabbit, cod fish-
cakes, asparagus or lamb, and the local wines.' The buffet
breakfast, 'well above Spanish average', includes tortilla and
fresh fruits. Tour coaches come to the attached cafeteria,
but the *parador* and its swimming area are off-limits to day
visitors.

Open All year. **Rooms** 2 suites, 34 double, 1 single. **Facilities**
Lounges, bar, café, restaurant. **Location** Centre of island, in
Cañadas del Teide national park. 70 km SW of Santa Cruz. **Credit
cards** All major cards accepted. **Terms** Room: single €81, double
€101. Breakfast €10. Set meals €24.

HOTEL EL PATIO   plantation

Finca Malpaís el Guincho
Garachico
38450 Tenerife
Canary Islands

Tel 00 34 922 13 32 80
Fax 00 34 922 83 00 89
Email reservas@hotelpatio.com
Website www.hotelpatio.com

On the peaceful north-west corner of Tenerife, above a lovely bay, this large banana plantation has been owned by the de Pontis family since 1507. They recently converted the ground floor of the *quinta*, and a nearby plantation building, into a small rural hotel: its central patio is filled with palm trees and centenarian dragon trees. Two glowing commendations: 'One of the most pleasant hotels I have visited. An oasis of calm in crowded Tenerife. The hands-on owners have successfully created a family atmosphere. Wonderful gardens all around: lots of places to sit and feel alone, and a swimming pool. The comfortable bedrooms deliberately have no TV or telephone.' 'Level of service and ambience exceptional. Almost every conceivable extra included in the very reasonable room rate.' You can walk through the banana trees to the coast. Guests who wish to dine order a fixed menu when taking the 'excellent' buffet breakfast. Garachico, nearby, has a variety of restaurants.

Open All year. **Rooms** 26 double. Some in annexe, 800 m. **Facilities** Lounges, 2 honesty bars, *bodega*, dining room. **Location** On coast, 3 km NE of Garachico. **Credit cards** All major cards accepted. **Terms** B&B: single €65–€80, double €75–€94, suite €91–€114. Set dinner €16.

HOTEL SAN ROQUE   stylish

Esteban de Ponte 32   *Tel* 00 34 922 13 34 35
Garachico   *Fax* 00 34 922 13 34 06
38450 Tenerife   *Email* info@hotelsanroque.com
Canary Islands   *Website* www.hotelsanroque.com

'Quite simply the best hotel we have stayed in.' 'Very pleasant and comfortable.' Praise from visitors to Laly and Dominique Carayon's stylish small hotel in a cobbled street near the seafront of this 'interesting little port', in the lush north-west of the island. A conversion of a 17th-century mansion, painted red, it has a Bauhaus interior with modern works of art, old woodwork, galleries, arcades and two patios: one has a futuristic steel sculpture, the other a swimming pool and tables where meals are served. 'Staff are attentive but not obtrusive.' Snr Carayon is 'a courteous man'; his son, also Dominique, is 'very chatty in perfect English'. Rooms vary in size: those on the first floor are 'worth the extra euros for space and *objets trouvés*'. Some rooms are a bit dark, some bathrooms are said to be 'awkwardly designed'. A no-choice three-course dinner can be served (book by 7 pm): 'We enjoyed duck, quail, bass, goat's cheese salad with ratatouille, wines from a well-chosen list.' 'An excellent buffet breakfast.'

Open All year. **Rooms** 4 suites, 14 double, 2 single. **Facilities** Salon/bar, restaurant. **Location** Centre of village on W end of N coast. Parking. **Credit cards** All major cards accepted. **Terms** B&B: single €145–€160, double €175–€200, suite €215–€243. Set dinner €25.

VALLADOLID
(Ryanair)

The airport, 12 km north-west of Valladolid,
provides access to the historic towns of the
Castilla y León region.

MESÓN DEL CID   Castilian

Plaza de Santa María 8	*Tel* 00 34 947 20 87 15
09003 Burgos	*Fax* 00 34 947 26 94 60

Email mesondelcid@mesondelcid.es
Website www.mesondelcid.es

The López Pascual family's 'good, pleasant hotel' is opposite
the great Gothic cathedral, where the medieval hero (El Cid)
lies buried, in Castile's ancient capital. Front bedrooms have
'superb views of the floodlit cathedral'; some rooms
overlook a narrow side street, which can be noisy. All have a
blend of antique and modern furnishings: 'Ours was simple,
but with a very good bathroom.' The Castilian cooking in the
restaurant is liked, but breakfast, in a 'canteen-like' room in
an adjoining building, is thought only 'adequate', and one
couple found the staff 'rather sullen'. A one-way system
makes access difficult, but 'there is help with luggage and
parking'.

Open All year. Restaurant closed 25 Dec, Sun night. **Rooms** 6
suites, 46 double, 3 single. **Facilities** Lift. Lounge, bar, restaurant.
Location Opposite cathedral. Private garage nearby; valet parking
(€12). **Credit cards** All major cards accepted. **Terms** Room:
single €92.50, double €115, suite €135. Breakfast €9. Set meals
€25.

POSADA DE LA CASA DEL ABAD   historic

Plaza Francisco Martín Gromaz 12   *Tel* 00 34 979 76 80 08
Ampudia   *Fax* 00 34 979 76 83 00
34191 Palencia   *Email* hotel@casadelabad.com
                                    Website www.casadelabad.com

In a small village with a mighty medieval fortress, the García Puertas family have converted their historic home, a listed 17th-century abbot's house, into a luxury hotel (Relais & Châteaux). One of the four sons was the architect; another is manager. There are bright colours and contemporary paintings. Recent visitors were impressed: 'An extraordinary mixture of ancient – beams, antiques, an old wine-press – and ultra modern: stainless steel washbasins and a spa bath in the bathroom (but the water ran slowly).' Guests may 'need a user's manual' to operate some of the hi-tech equipment, but a suite was thought 'agreeable'; its comfortable sitting room was supplied with champagne and pastries. The chef uses local produce 'to create surprises' in the restaurant, once the wine cellar ('exquisite christening robes on the wall'). A good buffet breakfast in a winter garden with tables made of old sewing machines. Staff 'charming if a bit stressed'.

Open All year. **Rooms** 6 suites, 11 double, 1 single. **Facilities** 3 salons, bar, winter garden, restaurant. **Location** Central. 20 km SW of Palencia. Garage, parking. **Credit cards** Amex, MasterCard, Visa. **Terms** Room: single €90–€100, double €110–€122, suite €148–€517. Breakfast €11. D,B&B €49 added per person.

PARADOR HOSTAL SAN MARCOS   palatial

Plaza de San Marcos 7
24001 León

Tel 00 34 987 23 73 00
Fax 00 34 987 23 34 58
Email leon@parador.es
Website www.parador.es

'Quite marvellous,' say visitors to León's remarkable *parador*, a former medieval monastery with an ornate Renaissance façade. Palatial public rooms have antiques and period furniture; tapestries soften cool stone walls; there is a beautiful cloister around a green courtyard, a chapter house and a museum. Most bedrooms are in a modern extension. Though large and well equipped, some may lack storage space. Some look over the river or garden, and are peaceful. Some suites in the historic main building overlook the main square. One guest recommended taking one of the two-bedroom, two-bathroom suites, which have 'a magnificent lounge' and will cost little more than two doubles. A 'great dinner, well served', was enjoyed in the large, brightly lit, modern dining room (reserving a table is advised). 'The usual good buffet breakfast.' Reception staff, as in many *paradores*, may be 'cool and businesslike'.

Open All year. **Rooms** 15 suites, 185 double. **Facilities** Lift, ramps. 13 salons, bar, restaurant, TV room. Garden. **Location** On river (signposted). Parking. **Credit cards** All major cards accepted. **Terms** Room: single €102–116, double €128–€145. Breakfast €10.50. Set meals €26.50.

SWEDEN

STOCKHOLM
(Ryanair)

Ryanair flies to Skavsta, 100 km south of the city,
and Västerås on Lake Mälaren, 50 km north-west.

BERNS HOTEL | contemporary

Näckströmsgatan 8 | *Tel* 00 46 8 566 32200
111 47 Stockholm | *Fax* 00 46 8 566 32201
| *Email* info@berns.se
| *Website* www.berns.se

Terence Conran was involved in the conversion of this
restaurant/bar complex, beside Berzelii Park, into a 'discreet
and exclusive' hotel. The centrepiece is the restaurant, an
ornate former 19th-century music hall, with huge mirrors
and chandeliers, contemporary paintings and fabrics, and oak
panelling. 'The food is typical Conran,' said a visitor who
enjoyed 'really good beefburgers'; oysters, smoked tuna and
rabbit are also on the menu. The bedrooms, which vary in
size, have a cool contemporary style, using cherry wood and
grey marble. 'Ours, on the roof, small, but beautifully done,
was like a ship's cabin.' 'Lavish breakfasts.'

Open All year, except Christmas week. Main restaurant closed
July. **Rooms** 3 suites, 43 double, 23 single. **Facilities** Salon,
cocktail bar, bar/grill, restaurant, terrace restaurant; nightclub.
Location Central, by Berzelii Park. **Credit cards** All major cards
accepted. **Terms** B&B: single 2,100 Skr, double 2,450–3,900 Skr,
suite 4,600–6,300 Skr.

LADY HAMILTON HOTEL   historic

Storkyrkobrinken 5
111 28 Stockholm

Tel 00 46 8 506 40100
Fax 00 46 8 506 40110
Email info@lady-hamilton.se
Website www.lady-hamilton.se

The Bengtsson family, Nelson enthusiasts, own a trio of hotels in the pedestrianised old town (Gamla Stan). Their philosophy is that 'hotel corridors should not be boring', and this conversion of three old houses near the cathedral and royal palace is 'like a mini-museum', said inspectors. A portrait by George Romney of Lady Hamilton as Bacchante hangs in the lobby, small wooden rocking horses and old wooden chests stand on landings, and there are collections of model ships, antique boxes, china and much more. Staff are 'friendly, though they don't go in for bag-carrying'. 'Our bedroom, at the top, had huge old beams, a wide seat under attic windows. Not much storage space, good shower room, smallish towels.' Some rooms face the street, 'charming but noisy'; top ones can be hot in summer. A self-service breakfast is served in a room hung with embroidered pictures of ships. Salads and sandwiches are available. The family also own the *Victory* and *Lord Nelson* ('Sweden's narrowest hotel').

Open All year. **Rooms** 16 double, 18 single. **Facilities** Lift. Lobby, bistro/breakfast room. **Location** Old town, by cathedral. Valet parking. **Restrictions** No smoking: bistro during breakfast, some bedrooms. **Credit cards** All major cards accepted. **Terms** B&B: single 1,090–2,190 Skr, double 1,690–2,690 Skr.

HOTELL LAURENTIUS character

Östra Strandvägen 12
Strängnäs
645 30 Södermanland

Tel 00 46 152 104 44
Fax 00 46 152 104 43
Email info@hotellaurentius.com
Website www.hotellaurentius.com

Jürgen Lüdtke, a 'transplanted Austrian who loves electronic gadgets', and his Swedish wife, Lena, are the 'congenial hosts' at this small B&B 'of character', an easy drive across Lake Mälaren from Västerås. 'They do all they can to give their guests a pleasant stay,' said a visitor. The converted dormitory of a girls' school stands opposite the steam-boat landing. 'On sunny days, most guests find a welcoming lawn chair near the host who entertains them with local history.' Breakfast is served al fresco in summer; on cold days it is in the Green Room (lounge), with fireplace and views of Ulfhäll bay. Public areas have books and magazines. Bedrooms, 'simple, clean, comfortable', are up flights of stairs off a hall. A restaurant is opposite; a small beach is nearby. In this old town are a 13th-century cathedral, Sweden's second school (founded 1626), and its first printing works.

Open All year. **Rooms** 9 double, 3 single. **Facilities** Breakfast room/lounge. **Location** Opposite pier, on Lake Mälaren. **Restriction** No smoking. **Credit cards** All major cards accepted. **Terms** B&B: single 595–850 Skr, double 895–1,095 Skr.

KRÄGGA HERRGÅRD   luxury

Bålsta   *Tel* 00 46 171 532 80
74693 Uppsala län   *Fax* 00 46 171 532 65
                                    Email info@kragga.se
                                    Website www.kragga.se

This 19th-century manor house stands on the shores of
Lake Mälaren, between the airport at Västerås and
Stockholm. Now a luxury hotel (Relais & Châteaux),
managed by its owner, Leif Bonér, it was found 'excellent' by
recent visitors. 'A warm welcome. The public rooms in the
manor house, filled with beautiful cut flowers, include a
charming library. Two modern wings enclose a lakeside
garden. Dinner was excellent; the lobster lasagne that came
with the halibut was perfect.' Other dishes include deer
steak with sausage of foie gras. 'Comprehensive wine list.
Breakfast good too.' In February you can walk or skate on
the frozen lake, 'unbelievably beautiful in the winter sun'.
The family also own *Thoresta Herrgård*, an 18th-century
manor house hotel at Bro, 10 kilometres to the south.

Open 2 Jan–26 Dec. Restaurant closed Sun. **Rooms** 4 suites, 39
double. **Facilities** Lounges, library, bar, restaurant. **Location**
Take Bålsta exit from E18 E of Västerås or NW of Stockholm.
Follow signs to Krågga. Parking. **Credit cards** All major cards
accepted. **Terms** B&B: double 1,200–2,000 Skr, suite from 2,900
Skr. Set lunch 165 Skr, dinner 610 Skr.

GOTHENBURG
(Ryanair)

The airport is 12 km north-west of the city.

HOTEL ROYAL   traditional

Drottninggatan 67   *Tel* 00 46 31 700 11 70
411 07 Gothenburg   *Fax* 00 46 31 700 11 79
                                  Email info@hotel-royal.com
                                  Website www.hotel-royal.com

One of the oldest hotels in Sweden (built 1852) has been
renovated by the Oddestad family, while preserving 19th-
century features such as the painted glass ceiling and original
cast-iron balustrade in the bright entrance hall. A family of
seven thought it 'a nice place'. Bedrooms are 'beautifully
done' ('ours had turquoise-painted furniture, a large
bathroom'), but there can be street noise, especially during
the *Kalas*, a festival/street party in August: quietest rooms
are at the back. 'Very good breakfast' in a 'plain but pleasant'
room. Free coffee, tea and home-baked biscuits are available
during the day.

Open All year, except Christmas/New Year. Restaurant closed
July and midday. **Rooms** 83. **Facilities** Lobby, breakfast room; tiny
courtyard. **Location** Near station and bus terminals. **Credit
cards** All major cards accepted. **Terms** B&B: single 690–1,195
Skr, double 890–1,395 Skr.

SWITZERLAND

GENEVA
(bmibaby, easyJet, FlyBE, Jet2)

The airport is in Switzerland, 6 km from the city;
but we recommend a nearby French retreat.

HÔTEL LE FARTORET   **budget**

Place de la Mairie, Éloise   *Tel* 00 33 4.50.48.07.18
Bellegarde-sur-Valserine   *Fax* 00 33 4.50.48.23.85
01200 Ain

Half an hour's drive from Geneva airport, this Relais du Silence/Logis de France is indeed quiet, apart from church bells. A collection of buildings, it is in a small hillside village amid fine scenery. The Bachmann-Gassilloud family owners, 'lovely warm people', create 'a happy atmosphere'. 'Both proprietors were much in evidence, and Madame, especially, is charming,' say visitors. 'The dining room is most attractive, large and airy with views to the Alps, and the service was impeccable. The set menu we chose was pricey, but worth it.' But the breakfast has recently come in for criticism: 'Packaged orange juice and indifferent coffee.' Some annexe bedrooms may be 'rather drab'.

Open All year, except Christmas/New Year. Closed Sun night low season. **Rooms** 38 double, 2 single. **Facilities** Lift. Salon, bar, restaurant; dining terrace. 5-hectare grounds: swimming pool. **Location** In Éloise. 5 km SE of Bellegarde, 35 km SW of Geneva. From A40, exit 11: 2 km towards Bellegarde. Garage. **Credit cards** All major cards accepted. **Terms** Room €38–€82. Breakfast €9.50. D,B&B €58–€116 per person.

ZÜRICH
(easyJet)

Kloten airport is 11 km north of Zürich.

ROMANTIK HOTEL FLORHOF   civilised

Florhofgasse 4
8001 Zürich

Tel 00 41 1 261 44 70
Fax 00 41 1 261 46 11
Email info@florhof.ch
Website www.florhof.ch

'Wonderfully old-fashioned, with most helpful reception staff.' 'A splendid place, quiet and civilised with helpful staff.' Praise in recent years for Brigitte and Beat Schiesser's 'delightful hotel', ten minutes' walk from the centre, amid quaint shops and good eating places. In the old part of the city, near the university, theatre and art museum, it is a listed 16th-century building, 'well furnished, quiet and comfortable, apart from distant sounds from the music department of the university (a bonus)'. Mixed reports on the food: 'Excellent but unduly expensive;' 'disappointing'. Breakfast is a buffet.

Open All year. Restaurant closed Christmas/New Year, Sat/Sun, bank holidays. **Rooms** 2 suites, 23 double, 10 single. **Facilities** Reading room, restaurant; terrace. Garden. **Location** Old town, near university. Parking. **Credit cards** All major cards accepted. **Terms** B&B: single 220–270 Sfrs, double 330–360 Sfrs, suite 470–570 Sfrs. Set lunch 42 Sfrs, dinner 85 Sfrs; alc 68–120 Sfrs.

GASTHOF HIRSCHEN AM SEE   lakeside

Seestrasse 856
Obermeilen
8706 Zürich

Tel 00 41 1 925 05 00
Fax 00 41 1 925 05 01
Email reservation@hirschen-meilen.ch
Website www.hirschen-meilen.ch

An attractive place to stay, well clear of the city's bustle, on Lake Zürich, 15 km south-east of the centre. 'Everything is most comfortable; staff are helpful,' writes a regular visitor. The bedrooms are 'delightfully furnished, with comfortable chairs and good lighting'. It's worth paying a little extra for one of the eight quiet ones that face the lake. No lounge area but there is a bar, an Italian taverna, and a French restaurant where the food was found 'quite splendid, the service professional'. Meals, including the 'excellent' buffet breakfast, are served on a waterside terrace in fine weather.

Open All year. Restaurant closed Mon Jan–Apr. **Rooms** 14 double, 2 single. **Facilities** Restaurant, bar, taverna. Terrace (meal service). **Location** On Lake Zürich, 15 km SE of Zürich towards Rapperswill. **Credit cards** All major cards accepted. **Terms** B&B: single 100–175 Sfrs, double 190–240 Sfrs, junior suite 275 Sfrs.